Congressional Research Service
Informing the legislative debate since 1914

The Military Commissions Act of 2009 (MCA 2009): Overview and Legal Issues

Jennifer K. Elsea
Legislative Attorney

August 4, 2014

Congressional Research Service
7-5700
www.crs.gov
R41163

CRS REPORT
Prepared for Members and
Committees of Congress

Summary

On November 13, 2001, President Bush issued a Military Order (M.O.) pertaining to the detention, treatment, and trial of certain non-citizens in the war against terrorism. Military commissions pursuant to the M.O. began in November 2004 against four persons declared eligible for trial, but the Supreme Court in *Hamdan v. Rumsfeld* invalidated the military commissions as improper under the Uniform Code of Military Justice (UCMJ). To permit military commissions to go forward, Congress approved the Military Commissions Act of 2006 (MCA), conferring authority to promulgate rules that depart from the strictures of the UCMJ and possibly U.S. international obligations. Military commissions proceedings were reinstated and resulted in three convictions under the Bush Administration.

Upon taking office in 2009, President Obama temporarily halted military commissions to review their procedures as well as the detention program at Guantánamo Bay in general, pledging to close the prison facilities there by January 2010, a deadline that passed unmet. One case was moved to a federal district court.

In May 2009, the Obama Administration announced that it was considering restarting the military commission system with some changes to the procedural rules. Congress enacted the Military Commissions Act of 2009 (MCA 2009) as part of the Department of Defense Authorization Act (NDAA) for FY2010, P.L. 111-84, to provide some reforms the Administration supported and to make other amendments to the Military Commissions Act, as described in this report. The plan to transfer five "high value detainees" to New York for trial in federal court, announced in November 2009, was halted due to resistance from Congress and some New York officials. Military commissions resumed under the new statute, resulting in an additional five convictions, although two of the previous convictions were reversed on appeal. The government was granted a rehearing *en banc* at the U.S. Court of Appeals for the D.C. Circuit for one case, which resulted in the partial reinstatement of a conspiracy conviction pending further review by the original panel of judges.

This report provides a background and analysis comparing military commissions as envisioned under the revised MCA to those established by the MCA 2006. After reviewing the history of the implementation of military commissions in the armed conflict against Al Qaeda and associated forces, the report provides an overview of the procedural safeguards provided in the MCA. Finally, the report provides two charts comparing the MCA as amended by the MCA 2009 to the original MCA enacted in 2006 and to general courts-martial. The first chart describes the composition and powers of the military tribunals, as well as their jurisdiction. The second chart, which compares procedural safeguards in courts-martial to the MCA as enacted and as amended, follows the same order and format used in CRS Report RL31262, *Selected Procedural Safeguards in Federal, Military, and International Courts*, as well as CRS Report R40932, *Comparison of Rights in Military Commission Trials and Trials in Federal Criminal Court*, both by Jennifer K. Elsea, to facilitate comparison with safeguards provided in federal court and international criminal tribunals.

Contents

Tables

Contacts

Introduction

The use of military commissions to try suspected terrorists has been the focus of intense debate (as well as significant litigation) since President Bush in November 2001 issued his original Military Order (M.O.) authorizing such trials.[1] The M.O. specified that persons subject to it would have no recourse to the U.S. court system to appeal a verdict or obtain any other sort of relief, but the Supreme Court essentially invalidated that provision in its 2004 opinion, *Rasul v. Bush*.[2] In response, Congress enacted the Detainee Treatment Act of 2005 (DTA).[3] The DTA did not authorize military commissions, but amended Title 28, *U.S. Code* to revoke all judicial jurisdiction over habeas claims by persons detained as "enemy combatants," and it created jurisdiction in the Court of Appeals for the District of Columbia Circuit to hear appeals of final decisions of military commissions.

The Supreme Court, after finding that Congress's efforts to strip it of jurisdiction did not apply to a case already pending before the Court, *Hamdan v. Rumsfeld*,[4] invalidated the military commission system established by presidential order. The Court held that although Congress had in general authorized the use of military commissions, such commissions were required to follow procedural rules as similar as possible to courts-martial proceedings, as required by the Uniform Code of Military Justice (UCMJ).[5] In response, Congress promptly passed the Military Commissions Act of 2006 (MCA 2006)[6] to authorize military commissions and establish procedural rules that were modeled after, but departed from in some significant ways, the UCMJ. The MCA 2006 also amended the Detainee Treatment Act in order to strip the judiciary of habeas

[1] Detention, Treatment, and Trial of Certain Non-Citizens in the War Against Terrorism §1(a), 66 *Federal Register* 57,833 (November 16, 2001) (hereinafter "M.O."). President Bush subsequently determined that 20 of the detainees at the U.S. Naval Station in Guantánamo Bay held in connection with the conflict were subject to the M.O., and 10 were eventually charged for trial before military commissions. *See* Press Release, Department of Defense, President Determines Enemy Combatants Subject to His Military Order (July 3, 2003), *available at* http://www.defense.gov/releases/release.aspx?releaseid=5511. According to the Defense Department, that determination is effectively "a grant of [military] jurisdiction over the person." *See* John Mintz, *6 Could Be Facing Military Tribunals*, WASH. POST, July 4, 2003, at A1. In 2004, nine additional detainees were determined to be eligible. *See* Press Release, Department of Defense, Presidential Military Order Applied to Nine More Combatants (July 7, 2004), *available at* http://www.defenselink mil/releases/release.aspx?releaseid=7525. In November 2005, five more detainees were charged. *See* Press Release, Department of Defense, Military Commission Charges Approved (November 7, 2005), *available at* http://www.defense.gov/releases/release.aspx?releaseid=9052.

[2] Rasul v. Bush, 542 U.S. 466 (2004). Persons subject to the M.O. were described as not privileged to "seek any remedy or maintain any proceeding, directly or indirectly" in federal or state court, the court of any foreign nation, or any international tribunal. M.O. at §7(b). However, the Bush Administration shortly thereafter indicated that defendants were not intended to be precluded from petitioning a federal court for a writ of habeas. *See* Alberto R. Gonzales, *Martial Justice, Full and Fair*, NY TIMES (op-ed), November 30, 2001. The government did not rely on the M.O. as the legal basis for asserting detainees had no right to pursue writs of habeas corpus, but the Court's opinion served as a warning that military commission verdicts would be subject to collateral review. For a summary of *Rasul* and related cases, see CRS Report R41156, *Judicial Activity Concerning Enemy Combatant Detainees: Major Court Rulings*, by Jennifer K. Elsea and Michael John Garcia.

[3] Title 10 of P.L. 109-148 and Title 14 of P.L. 109-163. The two versions of the Detainee Treatment Act (DTA) were identical as enacted, but subsequent amendments have resulted in some differences in the text.

[4] Hamdan v. Rumsfeld, 548 U.S. 557 (2006), *rev'g* 415 F.3d 33 (D.C. Cir. 2005).

[5] 10 U.S.C. §801 *et seq*. Military commissions were said to be authorized pursuant to 10 U.S.C. §§821 and 836.

[6] P.L. 109-366, 120 Stat. 2600, codified at chapter 47A of Title 10, *U.S. Code* (2006).

jurisdiction in all cases brought by detainees, including pending cases,[7] but the Supreme Court held that provision to be an unconstitutional suspension of the Writ of Habeas Corpus.[8]

President Bush reconstituted the military commissions under the MCA 2006 by issuing Executive Order 13425.[9] The Department of Defense (DOD) issued regulations for the conduct of military commissions pursuant to the MCA 2006[10] and restarted the military commission proceedings, which resulted in three convictions under the Bush Administration. One detainee, David Matthew Hicks of Australia, was convicted of material support to terrorism pursuant to a plea agreement in 2007.[11] In 2008, Salim Hamdan was found guilty of one count of providing material support for terrorism and sentenced to 66 months' imprisonment, but credited with five years' time served.[12] Both men are now free from detention. Ali Hamza Ahmad Suliman al Bahlul of Yemen was found guilty of multiple counts of conspiracy and solicitation to commit certain war crimes and of providing material support for terrorism in connection with his role as Al Qaeda's "propaganda chief."[13] He refused representation and boycotted most of his trial, and was subsequently sentenced to life imprisonment. The latter two convictions were reversed on appeal by the U.S. Court of Appeals for the D.C. Circuit.[14] The government sought and was granted a rehearing *en banc* in the *Bahlul* case to appeal the decisions. On rehearing, the D.C. Circuit invalidated Bahlul's convictions for solicitation and material support for terrorism on *ex post facto* grounds, but upheld the conspiracy charge, sending it back to the original panel to resolve additional challenges.[15]

No challenge to military commissions under the MCA 2006 reached the Supreme Court. President Obama halted the proceedings upon taking office in January 2009 in order to review whether to continue their use. The President issued an Executive Order requiring that the Guantánamo detention facility be closed no later than a year from the date of the Order.[16] The Order required specified officials to review all Guantánamo detentions to assess whether the detainee should continue to be held by the United States, transferred or released to another country, or be prosecuted by the United States for criminal offenses.[17] The Secretary of Defense

---

[7] P.L. 109-366 §7.

[8] Boumediene v. Bush, 533 U.S. 723 (2008). For an analysis of the case, see CRS Report R41156, *Judicial Activity Concerning Enemy Combatant Detainees: Major Court Rulings*, by Jennifer K. Elsea and Michael John Garcia.

[9] Exec. Ord. No. 13425, 72 *Federal Register* 7737 (February 14, 2007).

[10] Department of Defense, The Manual for Military Commissions ["M.M.C. 2007"], January 18, 2007, *available at* http://www.defenselink mil/news/MANUAL%20FOR%20MILITARY%20COMMISSIONS%202007%20signed.pdf.

[11] Press release, Department of Defense, Detainee Convicted of Terrorism Charge at Guantánamo Trial" (March 30, 2007), *available at* http://www.defenselink.mil/releases/release.aspx?releaseid=10678. Hicks was sentenced to seven years' confinement. As part of his pretrial agreement, his sentence was limited to nine months' confinement to be served in Australia, with six years and three months suspended.

[12] Press release, Department of Defense, Detainee Transfer Announced (November 28, 2008), *available at* http://www.defenselink mil/releases/release.aspx?releaseid=12372.

[13] Press release, Department of Defense, Detainee Sentenced To Life In Prison (November 3, 2008), *available at* http://www.defenselink mil/releases/release.aspx?releaseid=12331.

[14] Hamdan v. United States, 696 F.3d 1238 (D.C. Cir. 2012); Al Bahlul v. United States, 2013 WL 297726 (D.C. Cir. January 25, 2013) (per curiam).

[15] Al Bahlul v. United States, __ F3d. __ (D.C. Cir. 2014) (en banc). The court assumed without deciding that the protections of the Ex Post Facto Clause extend to a foreigner captured and held abroad.

[16] Exec. Ord. 13492, Review and Disposition of Individuals Detained at the Guantánamo Bay Naval Base and Closure of Detention Facilities, 74 *Federal Register* 4,897 (January 22, 2009).

[17] *Id.* at §4.

was also required to take steps to ensure that all proceedings before military commissions and the United States Court of Military Commission Review were halted, although some pretrial proceedings continued to take place. One case was moved to a federal district court.[18]

In May 2009, the Obama Administration announced that it was considering restarting the military commission system with some changes to the procedural rules.[19] DOD informed Congress about modifications to the Manual for Military Commissions, to take effect July 14, 2009.[20] The Senate passed the Military Commissions Act of 2009 (MCA 2009) as part of the Department of Defense Authorization Act (NDAA) for FY2010, S. 1391, to provide some reforms the Administration supported and to make other amendments to the Military Commissions Act, as described below. The bill that emerged from conference (H.R. 2647) contained some, but not all, of the proposals submitted by the Obama Administration, and was enacted October 28, 2009, P.L. 111-84.

President Obama's Detention Policy Task Force issued a preliminary report July 20, 2009, reaffirming that the White House considers military commissions to be an appropriate forum for trying some cases involving suspected violations of the laws of the war, although federal criminal court would be the preferred forum for trials of detainees.[21] The disposition of each case was assigned to a team composed of Department of Justice (DOJ) and Department of Defense (DOD) personnel, including prosecutors from the Office of Military Commissions. Appended to the report was a set of criteria to govern the disposition of cases involving Guantánamo detainees. This protocol identified three broad categories of factors to be taken into consideration:

- Strength of interest, namely, the nature and gravity of offenses or underlying conduct; identity of victims; location of offense; location and context in which the individual was apprehended; and the conduct of the investigation.
- Efficiency, namely, protection of intelligence source and methods; venue; number of defendants; foreign policy concerns; legal or evidentiary problems; efficiency and resource concerns.
- Other prosecution considerations, namely, the extent to which the forum and offenses that can be tried there permit a full presentation of the wrongful conduct, and the available sentence upon conviction.

Federal prosecutors are to evaluate their cases under "traditional principles of federal prosecution."

On November 13, 2009, Attorney General Holder announced his decision to transfer the five "9/11 conspirators," who include Khalid Sheikh Mohammed, Walid Muhammed Salih Mubarak Bin Attash, Ramzi Bin Al Shibh, Ali Abdul-Aziz Ali, and Mustafa Ahmed Al Hawsawi, to the

[18] Press Release, Department of Justice, Ahmed Ghailani Transferred from Guantánamo Bay to New York for Prosecution on Terror Charges (June 9, 2009), *available at* http://www.justice.gov/opa/pr/2009/June/09-ag-563.html. Ghailani was ultimately convicted and sentenced to life in prison. *See* Benjamin Weiser, *Ex-Detainee Gets Life Sentence in Embassy Blasts*, N.Y. TIMES, January 26, 2011, at A18. For more information, see CRS Report R41156, *Judicial Activity Concerning Enemy Combatant Detainees: Major Court Rulings*, by Jennifer K. Elsea and Michael John Garcia.

[19] Peter Finn, *Obama Set to Revive Military Commissions*, WASH. POST, May 9, 2009.

[20] Letter from Robert M. Gates, Secretary of Defense, to Senator Carl Levin, May 15, 2009.

[21] Memorandum from the Detention Policy Task Force to the Attorney General and the Secretary of Defense, July 20, 2009, http://www.scotusblog.com/wp-content/uploads/2009/07/law-of-war-prosecution-prelim-report-7-20-09.pdf.

Southern District of New York to stand trial.[22] Five other detainees to be tried by military commission included Omar Khadr, a Canadian citizen captured as a teenager and charged before a military commission for allegedly throwing a hand grenade that killed a U.S. soldier in Afghanistan;[23] Abd al-Rahim al-Nashiri, whose military commission charges related to the October 2000 attack on the USS *Cole* were previously withdrawn in February 2009; Ahmed Mohammed Ahmed Haza al Darbi, accused of participating in an Al Qaeda plot to blow up oil tankers in the Straits of Hormuz;[24] and two other detainees about whom no further information was given.[25]

As the deadline for closing the detention facility at Guantánamo passed unmet, the Obama Administration reportedly completed its assessment, determining that about 50 of the detainees held there would continue to be held without trial, that around 40 detainees would be prosecuted in military commission or federal court, and that the remaining 110 detainees would be released once a suitable country has agreed to take each of them.[26] However, the transfer of 30 detainees of Yemeni nationality was stymied because an Al Qaeda affiliate in Yemen is suspected to have been behind attempt to blow up a civilian airliner on Christmas Day 2009.[27]

---

[22] Press Release, U.S. Department of Justice, "Departments of Justice and Defense Announce Forum Decisions for Ten Guantánamo Detainees," November 13, 2009, *available at* http://www.justice.gov/opa/pr/2009/November/09-ag-1224 html.

[23] Khadr pleaded guilty in 2010 and was sentenced to 40 years in prison. He will serve eight years pursuant to his plea agreement, and has been transferred to Canada to serve the remaining portion of his sentence.

[24] Al Darbi pleaded guilty in February 2014 under an agreement that provides a sentence of between 13 and 15 years. *See* Charlie Savage, *Guantánamo Detainee Pleads Guilty in 2002 Attack on Tanker Off Yemen*, NY TIMES, February 20, 2014.

[25] One of these may have been Majid Shoukat Khan, who has pleaded guilty to conspiracy and other crimes in connection with the August 2003 bombing of the J.W. Marriot hotel in Indonesia and an attempted assassination of former Pakistani President Pervez Musharraf. The other may have been Noor Uthman Muhammed, who pleaded guilty to conspiracy and providing material support for terrorism in connection with service at the Khalden terrorist training camp in Afghanistan. He was sentenced in February 2011 to 14 years' imprisonment, but his plea agreement provided for only 34 months.

[26] *See* Charlie Savage, *Detainees Will Still Be Held, but Not Tried, Official Says*, NY TIMES, January 22, 2010.

[27] *Id.*

Table 1. Military Commissions: Completed Cases at Trial Level

Accused	Year of Verdict	Result	Charges	Post-military commission developments
David Hicks	2007	guilty plea	material support for terrorism	transferred to Australia to serve remainder of unsuspended portion (nine months) of seven-year sentence; has submitted new appeal to Court of Military Commissions Review (CMCR)
Salim Hamdan	2009	guilty finding	material support for terrorism, acquitted on conspiracy charge	overturned on appeal by the U.S. Court of Appeals for the D.C. Circuit
Ali al Bahlul	2009	guilty finding	conspiracy and providing material support for terrorism	convictions for material support and solicitation overturned by the U.S. Court of Appeals for the D.C. Circuit; conviction for conspiracy upheld
Ibrahim al-Qosi	2010	guilty plea	conspiracy and providing material support for terrorism	transferred to Sudan after serving two-year sentence with 12 years suspended; appellate counsel is seeking to appeal to CMCR
Omar Khadr	2010	guilty plea	murder and attempted murder in violation of the law of war, providing material support for terrorism, conspiracy, and spying	transferred to Canada to serve remainder of eight-year sentence; has submitted new appeal to CMCR
Noor Uthman Muhammed	2011	guilty plea	providing material support for terrorism and conspiracy	34 months' confinement pursuant to plea agreement, transferred to Sudan December 2013
Majid Shoukat Khan	2012	guilty plea	murder and attempted murder in violation of the law of war, providing material support for terrorism, spying and conspiracy	sentencing is delayed for four years, limited by plea agreement to 25 years' confinement
Ahmed Mohammed Ahmed Haza al Darbi	2014	guilty plea	conspiracy, attacking civilian objects, hazarding a vessel, terrorism, attempt, and aiding the enemy	sentencing is delayed for three years and six months, limited by plea agreement to 15 years' confinement

Source: Prepared by CRS from data derived from the Military Commissions website, http://www.mc.mil.

Military Commissions

Military commissions are courts usually set up by military commanders in the field to try persons accused of certain offenses during war.[28] They may also try persons for ordinary crimes during periods of martial law or military occupation, where regular civil courts are not able to function.[29] Past military commissions trying enemy belligerents for war crimes directly applied the international law of war, without recourse to domestic criminal statutes, unless such statutes were declaratory of international law.[30] Historically, military commissions have applied the same set of procedural rules that applied in courts-martial.[31] By statute, military commissions have long been available to try "offenders or offenses designated by statute or the law of war."[32] For the most part, military commissions have been employed where U.S. Armed Forces have established a military government or martial law, as in the war with Mexico, 1846-1848, the Civil War, the Philippine Insurrection of 1899-1902, and in occupied Germany and Japan after World War II.[33]

President Bush's Military Order setting up military commissions appeared to have been designed to replicate a pair of military commission orders issued during World War II by President Roosevelt for the trial of German saboteurs caught within the territory of the United States after having evaded U.S. coastal defenses. These tribunals were historically a bit anomalous in that they took place in Washington, DC, during a period when the civilian courts were open. A similar practice during the Civil War, which accounted for a small number of the military commission cases, was held unconstitutional. The Supreme Court held essentially in *Ex parte Milligan*[34] that military trials of persons who had never been members of the Armed Forces of the United States could never be valid on friendly territory where martial law has not been declared and civilian courts are functioning. However, the Supreme Court upheld the F.D.R. tribunals by explaining

---

[28] See CRS Report RL31191, *Terrorism and the Law of War: Trying Terrorists as War Criminals before Military Commissions*, by Jennifer K. Elsea (providing a general background of U.S. history of military commissions).

[29] *See* Hamdan v. Bush, 548 U.S. 557, 595 (2006). In looking at historical precedent, the *Hamdan* Court suggested, it is important to distinguish which type of jurisdiction a military commission is exercising, although the distinction is often blurred. *Id.* at 597 & note 7.

[30] *See* U.S. Army Field Manual (FM) 27-10, The Law of Land Warfare, Section 505(e) [hereinafter "FM 27-10"].

[31] *See* WILLIAM WINTHROP, MILITARY LAW AND PRECEDENTS 841-42 (2d ed. 1920)(noting that "in the absence of any statute or regulation," the same principles and procedures commonly govern, though possibly more "liberally construed and applied"); David Glazier, Note, *Kangaroo Court or Competent Tribunal?: Judging the 21st Century Military Commission*, 89 VA. L. REV. 2005 (2003).

[32] 10 U.S.C. §821. There are only two statutory offenses under the Uniform Code of Military Justice (UCMJ) for which convening a military commission is explicitly recognized: aiding the enemy and spying (in time of war). 10 U.S.C. §§904 and 906, respectively. The circumstances under which civilians accused of aiding the enemy may be tried by military tribunal have not been decided, but a court interpreting the article may limit its application to conduct committed in territory under martial law or military government, within a zone of military operations or area of invasion, or within areas subject to military jurisdiction. *See* FM 27-10, *supra* footnote 30, at para. 79(b)(noting that treason and espionage laws are available for incidents occurring outside of these areas, but are triable in civil courts); GEORGE B. DAVIS, A TREATISE ON THE MILITARY LAW OF THE UNITED STATES 417-18 (3d ed. 1913)(arguing that arts. 45 & 46 of the Articles of War, the precursors to 10 U.S.C. §§904 & 906, were essentially reliant on martial law to establish jurisdiction over civilians). Spying is not technically a violation of the law of war, but violates domestic law and traditionally may be tried by military commission. *See* FM 27-10, *supra* footnote 30, at para. 77 (explaining that spies are not punished as "violators of the law of war, but to render that method of obtaining information as dangerous, difficult, and ineffective as possible").

[33] For a review of military commission precedent, see David Glazier, *Precedents Lost: The Neglected History of the Military Commission*, 46 VA. J. INT'L L. 5 (2005).

[34] 71 U.S. (4 Wall.) 1 (1867).

that the holding in *Milligan* was limited to cases in which civilians—persons who are not members of the armed forces of an enemy government—were tried by military commission, and did not preclude the government from trying enemy belligerents for violations of the law of war, regardless of the operational status of the civilian courts.

The Bush Administration established rules prescribing detailed procedural safeguards for the tribunals.[35] These rules were praised as a significant improvement over what might have been permitted under the language of the M.O., but some continued to argue that the enhancements did not go far enough.[36] Critics also noted that the rules did not address the issue of indefinite detention without charge, as appeared to be possible under the original M.O.,[37] or that the Department of Defense may continue to detain persons who have been found not guilty by a military commission.[38] The Pentagon reportedly stated that its Inspector General (IG) looked into allegations, made by military lawyers assigned as prosecutors to the military commissions, that the proceedings were rigged to obtain convictions, but the IG did not substantiate the charges.[39]

The Military Commissions Act ("MCA")[40] grants the Secretary of Defense express authority to convene military commissions to prosecute those fitting the definition under the MCA of "alien unprivileged enemy belligerents."[41] The Secretary delegated the authority to a specially appointed "convening authority," who has responsibility for accepting or rejecting charges referred by the prosecution team, convening military commissions for trials, detailing military commission members and other personnel, approving requests from trial counsel to communicate with the media, approving requests for expert witnesses, approving plea agreements, carrying out post-trial reviews, and forwarding cases for review, along with other duties spelled out in the MCA or in DOD's Regulation for Trial by Military Commission.[42]

The MCA eliminates the requirement for military commissions to conform to either of the two uniformity requirements in article 36, UCMJ, which President Bush's military commissions were

---

[35] Military Commission Order No. 1 ("M.C.O. No. 1"), *reprinted at* 41 I.L.M. 725 (2002). A revision was issued August 31, 2005. The Department of Defense (DOD) subsequently released ten "Military Commission Instructions" ("M.C.I. No. 1-10") to elaborate on the set of procedural rules to govern military tribunals. The instructions set forth the elements of some crimes to be tried by military commission, established guidelines for civilian attorneys, and provided other administrative guidance and procedures for military commissions. These historical documents can be found at http://www mc mil/LEGALRESOURCES/MilitaryCommissionsDocuments/HistoricalDocuments.aspx.

[36] *See* ACTL, Supplemental Report on Military Commissions for the Trial of Terrorists, October 2005, online at http://www.actl.com/AM/Template.cfm?Section=Home&template=/CM/ContentDisplay.cfm&ContentID=2152.

[37] The Bush Administration did not explicitly use this authority; instead, it characterized the prisoners as "enemy combatants" detained pursuant to the law of war. *See, e.g.*, Response of the United States to Request for Precautionary Measures - Detainees in Guantánamo Bay, Cuba to the Inter-American Commission on Human Rights, Organization of American States 25 (2002)("It is humanitarian law, and not human rights law, that governs the capture and detention of enemy combatants in an armed conflict.")

[38] *See* Bruce Zagaris, *U.S. Defense Department Issues Order on Military Commissions*, 18 No. 5 INT'L ENFORCEMENT L. REP 215 (2002) (citing comments by former DOD chief counsel William J. Haynes II to a New York Times reporter).

[39] *See* Neil A. Lewis, *Two Prosecutors Faulted Trials for Detainees*, NY TIMES, August 1, 2005, at A1.

[40] P.L. 111-84 at codified as amended at chapter 47a of Title 10, *U.S. Code*. Unless otherwise noted, the terms "Military Commissions Act" or "MCA" (without specifying the year enacted) in this report refer to the 2009 version of the act as codified in Title 10.

[41] 10 U.S.C. §948h and 948c.

[42] Available at http://www.defenselink mil/news/Apr2007/Reg_for_Trial_by_mcm.pdf. The latest version of the regulation was published in 2011 and is available at http://www mc mil/Portals/0/2011%20Regulation.pdf.

held in *Hamdan* to violate. Instead, it establishes chapter 47A in Title 10, *U.S. Code* and excepts military commissions under this chapter from the requirements in article 36.[43] It provides that the UCMJ "does not, by its terms, apply to trial by military commissions except as specifically provided in this chapter." While declaring that the enacted chapter is "based upon the procedures for trial by general courts-martial under [the UCMJ]," it establishes that "[t]he judicial construction and application of [the UCMJ], while instructive, is therefore not of its own force binding on military commissions established under this chapter."[44] It expressly exempts these military commissions from UCMJ articles 10 (speedy trial), 31 (self-incrimination warnings), and 32 (pretrial investigations),[45] and the MCA 2006 amended articles 21, 28, 48, 50(a), 104, and 106 of the UCMJ to except military commissions under chapter 47A.[46] Other provisions of the UCMJ are to apply to trial by military commissions under chapter 47A only to the extent provided therein.[47]

Jurisdiction

The MCA establishes jurisdiction for military commissions somewhat more narrowly than that asserted in President Bush's M.O. The M.O. was initially criticized by some as overly broad in its assertion of jurisdiction, because it could be interpreted to cover non-citizens who had no connection with Al Qaeda or the terrorist attacks of September 11, 2001, as well as offenders or offenses not triable by military commission pursuant to statute or the law of war.[48] A person designated by President Bush as subject to his M.O. was amenable to detention and possible trial by military tribunal for violations of the law of war and "other applicable law."[49] The MCA 2006 largely validated President Bush's jurisdictional scheme for military commissions.

Jurisdiction over the Offender

The MCA, as amended in 2009, authorizes military commissions to try any "alien unprivileged enemy belligerent," which includes an individual (other than a privileged belligerent)[50] who:

> (A) has engaged in hostilities against the United States or its coalition partners;

[43] MCA 2006 §4 (adding to 10 U.S.C. §836(a) the words "except as provided in chapter 47A of this title" and to §836(b) the words "except insofar as applicable to military commissions established under chapter 47A of this title").

[44] 10 U.S.C. §948b.

[45] 10 U.S.C. §948b(d).

[46] MCA 2006 §4 (amending 10 U.S.C. §§821(jurisdiction of general courts-martial not exclusive), 828 (detail or employment of reporters and interpreters), 848 (power to punish contempt), 850(a) (admissibility of records of courts of inquiry), 904 (aiding the enemy), and 906 (spying)). The 2009 MCA amendments, Title XVIII of P.L. 111-84, enable military commissions under chapter 47A to try alien enemy unprivileged belligerents for violating 10 U.S.C. §§904 and 906, but did not amend 10 U.S.C. §§904 & 906 to reflect the change.

[47] 10 U.S.C. §948b(d)(2).

[48] For a discussion of criticism related to the M.O. and M.C.O. No. 1, see CRS Report RL31600, *The Department of Defense Rules for Military Commissions: Analysis of Procedural Rules and Comparison with Proposed Legislation and the Uniform Code of Military Justice*, by Jennifer K. Elsea; NATIONAL INSTITUTE OF MILITARY JUSTICE, ANNOTATED GUIDE: PROCEDURES FOR TRIALS BY MILITARY COMMISSIONS OF CERTAIN NON-UNITED STATES CITIZENS IN THE WAR AGAINST TERRORISM 10-11(2004)(hereinafter "NIMJ").

[49] M.O. §1(e) (finding such tribunals necessary to protect the United States and for effective conduct of military operations).

[50] A privileged belligerent is defined " an individual belonging to one of the eight categories enumerated in Article 4 of the Geneva Convention Relative to the Treatment of Prisoners of War," 10 U.S.C. §948a(6).

> (B) has purposefully and materially supported hostilities against the United States or its coalition partners; or
>
> (C) was a part of Al Qaeda at the time of the alleged offense under [chapter 47A of Title 10, *U.S. Code*].[51]

Thus, persons who do not directly participate in hostilities, but "purposefully and materially" support hostilities, are subject to trial under the MCA.[52] Citizens who fit the definition of "unprivileged enemy belligerent" are not amenable to trial by military commission under the MCA, but their detention is not expressly precluded.[53]

The MCA, as amended, defines "hostilities" to mean any conflict "subject to the laws of war."[54] It does not explain what conduct amounts to "supporting hostilities." To the extent that the jurisdiction is interpreted to include conduct that falls outside the accepted definition of participation in an armed conflict, the MCA might run afoul of the courts' historical aversion to trying civilians before military tribunals when other courts are available.[55] It is unclear whether this principle would apply to aliens captured and detained overseas, but the MCA does not appear to exempt from military jurisdiction permanent resident aliens captured in the United States who might otherwise meet the definition of "unprivileged enemy belligerent." It is generally accepted that aliens within the United States are entitled to the same protections in criminal trials that apply to U.S. citizens. Therefore, to subject persons to trial by military commission who do not meet the exception carved out by the Supreme Court in *ex parte Quirin*[56] for unlawful belligerents, to the extent such persons enjoy constitutional protections, would likely raise significant constitutional questions. To date, no resident aliens have been charged for trial before a military commission under the MCA.

As originally enacted, the MCA 2006 did not specifically identify who was to make the determination that defendants met the definition of "unlawful enemy combatant." The government sought to establish jurisdiction based on the determinations of Combatant Status Review Tribunals (CSRTs), set up by the Pentagon to determine the status of detainees using procedures similar to those the Army uses to determine POW status during traditional wars.[57] The

---

[51] 10 U.S.C. §948a(7). Prior to the 2009 amendment, any alien "unlawful enemy combatant" was subject to jurisdiction, which was defined to mean:

> (i) a person who has engaged in hostilities or who has purposefully and materially supported hostilities against the United States or its co-belligerents who is not a lawful enemy combatant (including a person who is part of the Taliban, Al Qaeda, or associated forces); or
>
> (ii) a person who, before, on, or after the date of the enactment of the Military Commissions Act of 2006, has been determined to be an unlawful enemy combatant by a Combatant Status Review Tribunal or another competent tribunal established under the authority of the President or the Secretary of Defense.

Previous 10 U.S.C. §948a(1).

[52] The definition applies to military commission jurisdiction, and does not describe who can be detained under the AUMF.

[53] For analysis of the authority to detain U.S. citizens, see CRS Report R42337, *Detention of U.S. Persons as Enemy Belligerents*, by Jennifer K. Elsea

[54] 10 U.S.C. §948a(9).

[55] *See, e.g., Ex parte* Milligan, 71 U.S. (4 Wall.) 2 (1866); Duncan v. Kahanamoku, 327 U.S. 304 (1945).

[56] 317 U.S. 1 (1942).

[57] *See* Department of Defense (DOD) Fact Sheet, "Combatant Status Review Tribunals," *available at* http://www.defenselink mil/news/Jul2004/d20040707factsheet.pdf. CSRT proceedings are modeled on the procedures (continued...)

CSRTs, however, were not empowered to determine whether the enemy combatants are unlawful or lawful, which led two military commission judges to hold that CSRT determinations are inadequate to form the basis for the jurisdiction of military commissions.[58] The Court of Military Commission Review (CMCR) reversed.[59] While it agreed that the CSRT determinations are insufficient by themselves to establish jurisdiction, it found the military judge erred in declaring that the status determination had to be made by a competent tribunal other than the military commission itself.

In denying the government's request to find that CSRT determinations are sufficient to establish jurisdiction over the accused, the CMCR interpreted the MCA to require more than establishing membership in Al Qaeda or the Taliban. The CMCR found

> no support for [the government's] claim that Congress, through the M.C.A., created a "comprehensive system" which sought to embrace and adopt all prior C.S.R.T. determinations that resulted in "enemy combatant" status assignments, and summarily turn those designations into findings that persons so labeled could also properly be considered "unlawful enemy combatants." Similarly, we find no support for [the government's] position regarding the parenthetical language contained in § 948a(1)(A)(i) of the M.C.A.—"including a person who is part of the Taliban, Al Qaeda, or associated forces." We do not read this language as declaring that a member of the Taliban, Al Qaeda, or associated forces is *per se* an "unlawful enemy combatant" for purposes of exercising criminal jurisdiction before a military commission. We read the parenthetical comment as simply elaborating upon the sentence immediately preceding it. That is, that a member of the Taliban, Al Qaeda, or associated forces *who has engaged in hostilities or who has purposefully and materially supported hostilities against the United States or its co-belligerents* will also qualify as an "unlawful enemy combatant" under the M.C.A. (emphasis added [by the court]).[60]

As a consequence of the decision, the prosecution has the burden of proving jurisdiction over each person charged for trial by a military commission. The Manual for Military Commissions was amended in May 2009 to reflect this practice,[61] and the 2009 MCA amended 10 U.S.C. Section 948d to task the military commission with establishing its own jurisdiction. Under the amended language, membership in Al Qaeda (but not the Taliban) appears sufficient to establish jurisdiction, regardless of whether the defendant participated in or even supported hostilities, although the defendant must generally be alleged to have committed one of the listed crimes "in the context of and associated with hostilities."[62]

(...continued)

of Army Regulation (AR) 190-8, Enemy Prisoners of War, Retained Personnel, Civilian Internees and Other Detainees (1997), which establishes administrative procedures to determine the status of detainees under the Geneva Conventions and prescribes their treatment in accordance with international law. It does not include a category for "unlawful" or "enemy" combatants, who would presumably be covered by the other categories.

[58] *See* Josh White and Shailagh Murray, *Guantánamo Ruling Renews the Debate Over Detainees*, WASH. POST, June 6, 2007, at A3.

[59] United States v. Khadr, 717 F. Supp. 2d 1215 (USCMCR 2007).

[60] *Id.* at 1228. The statutory language defining who can be tried was altered by the MCA 2009. *See supra,* footnote 51.

[61] Gates letter, *supra* footnote 20.

[62] 10 U.S.C. §950p(c).

Subject Matter Jurisdiction

The MCA provides jurisdiction to military commissions to try alien unprivileged belligerents for listed offenses as well as Sections 904 and 906 of Title 10 (aiding the enemy and spying), or the law of war, "whether such offense was committed before, on, or after September 11, 2001."[63] Crimes to be triable by military commission are defined in subchapter VIII (10 U.S.C. §§950p–950t). The MCA defines the following offenses: murder of protected persons; attacking civilians, civilian objects, or protected property; pillaging; denying quarter; taking hostages; employing poison or similar weapons; using protected persons or property as shields; torture, cruel or inhuman treatment; intentionally causing serious bodily injury; mutilating or maiming; murder in violation of the law of war; destruction of property in violation of the law of war; using treachery or perfidy; improperly using a flag of truce or distinctive emblem; intentionally mistreating a dead body; rape; sexual assault or abuse; hijacking or hazarding a vessel or aircraft; terrorism; providing material support for terrorism; wrongfully aiding the enemy; spying; attempts; conspiracy; solicitation; contempt; perjury and obstruction of justice.

The MCA largely adopted the list of offenses DOD had authorized for trial by military commission under the presidential order.[64] That list was not meant to be exhaustive. Rather, it was intended as an illustration of acts punishable under the law of war[65] or triable by military commissions.[66] The regulations contained an express prohibition of trials for *ex post facto* crimes.[67]

Although many of the crimes defined in the MCA seem to be well established offenses against the law of war, at least in the context of an international armed conflict,[68] some of the listed crimes

[63] 10 U.S.C. §948d.

[64] Military Commission Instruction (M.C.I.) No. 2, Crimes and Elements for Trials by Military Commission. M.C.I. No. 2 was published in draft form by DOD for outside comment. The final version appears to have incorporated some of the revisions, though not all, suggested by those who offered comments. *See* NATIONAL INSTITUTE OF MILITARY JUSTICE, MILITARY COMMISSION INSTRUCTIONS SOURCEBOOK 95 (2003) [hereinafter "SOURCEBOOK"].

[65] Crimes against the law of war listed in M.C.I. No. 2 were: (1) Willful Killing of Protected Persons; (2) Attacking Civilians; (3) Attacking Civilian Objects; (4) Attacking Protected Property; (5) Pillaging; (6) Denying Quarter; (7) Taking Hostages; (8) Employing Poison or Analogous Weapons; (9) Using Protected Persons as Shields; (10) Using Protected Property as Shields; (11) Torture; (12) Causing Serious Injury; (13) Mutilation or Maiming; (14) Use of Treachery or Perfidy; (15) Improper Use of Flag of Truce; (16) Improper Use of Protective Emblems; (17) Degrading Treatment of a Dead Body; and (18) Rape.

[66] Crimes "triable by military commissions" included (1) Hijacking or Hazarding a Vessel or Aircraft; (2) Terrorism; (3) Murder by an Unprivileged Belligerent; (4) Destruction of Property by an Unprivileged Belligerent; (5) Aiding the Enemy; (6) Spying; (7) Perjury or False Testimony; and (8) Obstruction of Justice Related to Military Commissions. Listed as "other forms of liability and related offenses" are: (1) Aiding or Abetting; (2) Solicitation; (3) Command/Superior Responsibility - Perpetrating; (4) Command/Superior Responsibility - Misprision; (5) Accessory After the Fact; (6) Conspiracy; and (7) Attempt.

[67] *See* M.C.I. No. 2 §3(A) ("No offense is cognizable in a trial by military commission if that offense did not exist prior to the conduct in question.").

[68] International armed conflicts are governed primarily by the Hague Convention No. IV Respecting the Laws and Customs of War on Land, October 18, 1907, 36 Stat. 2277 ("Hague Convention"), and the Geneva Conventions.

Non-international armed conflicts are not covered by the Hague Convention, and are covered only by Common Article 3 of the Geneva Conventions. However, some international criminal tribunals have worked to define war crimes applicable in non-international armed conflicts. For example, Article 3 of the Statute governing the International Criminal Tribunal for the former Yugoslavia (ICTY) includes the following as violations of the laws or customs of war in non-international armed conflict.

Such violations shall include, but not be limited to:

(continued...)

may be new. For example, a plurality of the Supreme Court in *Hamdan* agreed that conspiracy is not a war crime under the traditional law of war.[69] The crime of "murder in violation of the law of war," which punishes persons who commit hostile acts that result in the death of any persons, including lawful combatants, may also be new, depending on how it is interpreted. The Department of Defense had argued that the element "in violation of the law of war" is established by showing that the perpetrator is an unprivileged belligerent.[70] The latest version of the Manual for Military Commissions[71] reflects the understanding that the offense may be tried by military commission even if it does not violate the international law of war.[72]

While it appears to be well established that a civilian who kills a lawful combatant is triable for murder and cannot invoke the defense of combatant immunity,[73] it is not clear that the murder

(...continued)

> (a) employment of poisonous weapons or other weapons calculated to cause unnecessary suffering;
>
> (b) wanton destruction of cities, towns or villages, or devastation not justified by military necessity;
>
> (c) attack, or bombardment, by whatever means, of undefended towns, villages, dwellings, or buildings;
>
> (d) seizure of, destruction or wilful damage done to institutions dedicated to religion, charity and education, the arts and sciences, historic monuments and works of art and science;
>
> (e) plunder of public or private property.

UN Doc. S/Res/827 (1993), art. 3. The ICTY Statute and procedural rules are available at http://www.un.org/icty/legaldoc-e/index htm. The Trial Chamber in the case Prosecutor v. Naletilic and Martinovic, (IT-98-34)March 31, 2003, interpreted Article 3 of the Statute to cover specifically: "(i) violations of the Hague law on international conflicts; (ii) infringements of provisions of the Geneva Conventions other than those classified as grave breaches by those Conventions; (iii) violations of [Common Article 3] and other customary rules on internal conflicts, and (iv) violations of agreements binding upon the parties to the conflict" *Id.* at para. 224. *See also* Prosecutor v. Tadic, (IT-94-1) (Appeals Chamber), Decision on the Defence Motion for Interlocutory Appeal on Jurisdiction, October 2, 1995, para. 86-89.

The Appeals Chamber there set forth factors that make an offense a "serious" violation necessary to bring it within the ICTY's jurisdiction:

> (i) the violation must constitute an infringement of a rule of international humanitarian law;
>
> (ii) the rule must be customary in nature or, if it belongs to treaty law, the required conditions must be met ...
>
> (iii) the violation must be "serious," that is to say, it must constitute a breach of a rule protecting important values, and the breach must involve grave consequences for the victim....
>
> (iv) the violation of the rule must entail, under customary or conventional law, the individual criminal responsibility of the person breaching the rule.

Id. at para. 94.

[69] Hamdan v. Rumsfeld, 548 U.S. 557, 611 (2006). That this finding did not command a majority of Justices led the D.C. Circuit to uphold a conviction for conspiracy by a military commission under a "plain error" standard. Al Bahlul v. United States, __ F3d. __ (D.C. Cir. 2014).

[70] M.M.C. 2007, *supra* footnote 10, at IV-11-12. The comment on the crime "intentionally causing serious bodily injury" stated that "For the accused to have been acting in violation of the law of war, the accused must have taken acts as a combatant without having met the requirements for lawful combatancy." With respect to the crime "destruction of property in violation of the law of war," the M.M.C. stated that "A 'violation of the law of war' may be established by proof of the status of the accused as an unlawful combatant or by proof of the character of the property destroyed, or both." *Id.* at IV-13.

[71] Department of Defense, Manual for Military Commissions 2012 (M.M.C. 2012).

[72] *Id.* at IV-14 (comment to the crime of murder in violation of the law of war). Oddly, that the killing "was in violation of the law of war" remains an element of the offense. *Id.*

[73] Civil War records contain many examples of military commission cases against persons who, although not members of "any lawfully organized or authorized force at war with the United States," participated in the killing of other (continued...)

constitutes a violation of the law of war (rather than domestic or martial law),[74] or that the same principle applies in armed conflicts of a non-international nature, where combatant immunity does not apply.[75] The International Criminal Tribunal for the former Yugoslavia (ICTY) has found that war crimes in the context of non-international armed conflict include murder of protected persons, but has found that the killing of a combatant is not necessarily a war crime.[76] Thus, prison guards at Omarska and other detention camps were found guilty, among other crimes, of "murder, as a violation of the laws or customs of war" for causing the deaths of prisoners.[77] Similarly, the International Criminal Court applies a definition of murder in the context of a non-international armed conflict to require that the victim is a protected person,[78] while the killing (or wounding) of a "combatant adversary" is defined as a war crime only if it is done "treacherously."[79]

While one of the Guantánamo military commission judges found, without elaborating on what "murder in violation of the law of war" entails, that Congress could reasonably conclude that it

(...continued)

persons, including soldiers, "contrary to the laws and customs of war." *See, e.g.* Trial of Smith Crim, General Order (G.O.) 151, May 26, 1863 (trial of civilian in Missouri for murder of a U.S. Army officer); Trial of Thomas J. Caldwell and others, G.O. 267, August 3, 1863 (trial of guerrilla for murder of U.S. soldier as well as loyal citizens in Missouri). However, the fact that specifications of the charges often included reference to the defendant being "a citizen of the United States and owing allegiance thereto" or that the act took place "within the lines occupied by the lawfully authorized military force of the United States" suggests that the actual legal basis for the charge was a state of martial law or military occupation rather than the law of war as it applies to belligerents.

[74] *See, generally*, David R. Frakt, *Direct Participation in Hostilities as a War Crime: America's Failed Efforts to Change the Law of War*, 46 VAL. U. L. REV. 729 (2012).

[75] The U.S. Civil War was considered to be governed by the rules of international warfare as far as combatant immunity and related concepts were concerned. *See, e.g.*, Trial of T.E. Hogg and others, G.O. 52, HQ, Department of the Pacific, June 27, 1865, *reprinted in* [Series II] 7 WAR OF THE REBELLION: OFFICIAL RECORDS OF THE UNION AND CONFEDERATE ARMIES ("OFFICIAL RECORDS") 674, 677 (1899) ("[C]ivil wars are not distinguishable from other wars as to belligerent and neutral rights ... in such contests the principles of public law in relation to belligerents must govern, and all the rights which a state of war gives to public enemies are to be allowed to the respective parties engaged in them.")(quoting "Stevenson to Palmerston"); General Order No. 1, HQ, Dept. of the Missouri, January 1, 1862, *reprinted in* [Series I] 8 OFFICIAL RECORDS at 476-78. With respect to the current conflict against Al Qaeda, the Supreme Court in *Hamdan* held that Common Article 3 applies, interpreting "conflict not of an international nature" in the definition "in contradistinction to a conflict between nations," which the Geneva Conventions designate a "conflict of international character." 548 U.S. 557, 630 (2006).

[76] *See, e.g.*, Prosecutor v. Pavle Strugar, Case No. It-01-42-A (Appeals Chamber), Judgment, July 17, 2008, para. 172 ("In order to prove cruel treatment as a violation of Common Article 3 ... the Prosecution must prove beyond a reasonable doubt that the victim of the alleged offence was a person taking no active part in the hostilities"); Prosecutor v. Kvocka *et al.*, Case No. IT-98-30/1 (Trial Chamber), November 2, 2001, para. 124: ("An additional requirement for Common Article 3 crimes under Article 3 of the Statute is that the violations must be committed against persons 'taking no active part in the hostilities.'"), *aff'd.* Case No. IT-98-30/1-A (Appeals Chamber), February 28, 2005; Prosecutor v. Jelisic, Case No. IT-95-10 (Trial Chamber), December 14, 1999, para. 34 (Common Article 3 protects "[p]ersons taking no active part in the hostilities" including persons "placed *hors de combat* by sickness, wounds, detention, or any other cause."); Prosecutor v. Blaskic, Case No. IT-95-14 (Trial Chamber), March 3, 2000, para. 180 ("Civilians within the meaning of Article 3 are persons who are not, or no longer, members of the armed forces. Civilian property covers any property that could not be legitimately considered a military objective.").

[77] Prosecutor v. Kvocka *et al.* (The elements of the "murder" offense vary depending on whether it is charged as a violation of the laws and customs of war or a crime against humanity).

[78] *See* KNUT DÖRMANN, ELEMENTS OF WAR CRIMES UNDER THE ROME STATUTE OF THE INTERNATIONAL CRIMINAL COURT 383 (2003) (describing elements common to crimes under article 8(2)(c) of the Rome Statute of the International Criminal Court).

[79] *See id.* at 476 (describing elements of "killing or wounding treacherously a combatant adversary" under article 8(2)(e)(ix) of the Rome Statute).

constitutes a common law violation of the law of war,[80] another read the crime to consist of two elements: "the [attempted] killings ... were committed by an unlawful enemy combatant AND (2) that the method, manner or circumstances used violated the law of war."[81] There is historical support for the view that the offense pertains to means and methods of killing, but the notion that the unlawfulness element may be satisfied by proof that the offender is an "unlawful combatant" is not well supported. Military commissions were used during the U.S. Civil War to try the charge of "murder in violation of the law of war," but this charge apparently applied to *privileged belligerents* who committed murder perfidiously or who killed prisoners of war,[82] while unprivileged belligerents were charged simply with murder.[83] The charge of "murder, in violation of the laws of war" was occasionally brought against Filipino natives during the Philippine Insurrection, generally involving the killing of unarmed civilians or prisoners.[84] However, it is not easy to discern why some cases were charged as "murder" while others had added the phrase "in violation of the laws of war."[85] Sometimes the distinction appears to turn on the status of the victim, other times the determining factor seems to be the status of the perpetrator or more precisely, the authority under which the hostile act was carried out. Murder qualified by reference to the law of war was charged most frequently against those whose legitimacy as combatants was not challenged. In one case in which insurgents killed U.S. soldiers during a firefight, the conviction for murder in the violation of the laws of war was overturned in part on the basis that

[80] United States v. Khadr, Ruling on Defense Motion to Dismiss Charge One for Failure to State an Offense and for Lack of Subject Matter Jurisdiction (D-008) (April 21, 2008).

[81] United States v. Jawad, Ruling on Defense Motion to Dismiss—Lack of Subject Matter Jurisdiction (D-007) (September 24, 2008) (rejecting prosecution argument that 'murder in violation of the law of war' is identical to the charge of 'murder by an unprivileged belligerent'). Two other judges reached similar conclusions. *See* U.S. Congress, House Committee on the Judiciary, Subcommittee on the Constitution, Civil Rights, and Civil Liberties, *Proposals for Reform of the Military Commissions System*, 111th Cong., 1st sess., June 30, 2006 (prepared testimony of former Guantánamo military defense attorney Maj. David Frakt, USAFR).

[82] *See* CHARLES ROSCOE HOWLAND, A DIGEST OF OPINIONS OF THE JUDGE ADVOCATES GENERAL OF THE ARMY, 1071-72 (1912); *id.* at 1072 & note 1 (noting that 1873 military commission trying Modoc Indians for 'a treacherous killing of an enemy during a truce' charged the offense as "murder in violation of the law of war"); Trial of Henry Wirz, General Court Martial Order (G.C.M.O.) no. 607, November 6, 1865, *reprinted in* [Series II] 8 OFFICIAL RECORDS OF THE UNION AND CONFEDERATE ARMIES 784, 786 (1899) (Confederate officer charged for "murder in violation of the laws and customs of war" for shooting death of prisoner of war); Trial of James W. Duncan, G.C.M.O. 153, June 8, 1866 *reprinted in* [Series II] 8 OFFICIAL RECORDS 926 (1899) (employee "in the rebel military service" charged with "murder in violation of the laws of war" for beating death of prisoner).

[83] *See* cases listed *supra* note 73; Trial of Frank B. Gurley, G.C.M.O. no. 505, September 6, 1865, *reprinted in* [Series II] 8 OFFICIAL RECORDS 741 (Judge Advocate General approved conviction of "citizen" not "lawfully in the services of the so-called Confederate States" for murder of U.S. general officer where accused could not provide proof of Confederate commission). Gurley was, despite his death sentence, exchanged as a prisoner of war, to the consternation of the Judge Advocate General, *see id.* at 742. Military commission trials of persons not in the service of the Confederate government, including those tried for guerrilla activities in during periods of martial law, were later held invalid by civil courts on the basis that civil courts were open when the trials took place. *In re* Murphy, 17 F. Cas. 1030 (1867); District Court v. Commandant of Fort Delaware, 25 F. Cas. 590 (1866); *In re* Egan, 8 F. Cas. 367 (1866); Thompson v. Wharton, 70 Ky. 563 (Ky. 1870). Military detention of such persons without trial was also held to be unlawful. Johnson v. Jones, 44 Ill. 142 (Ill. 1867); Carver v. Jones, 45 Ill. 334 (Ill. 1867).

[84] For military commission trials against Filipinos for cruelty to U.S. soldiers, see U.S. Congress, Senate Committee on the Philippines, *Affairs in the Philippine Islands*, 57th Cong., 1st sess., April 10, 1902, S.Hrg. 57-331, 1340 *et seq.* (Washington: GPO, 1902). Sometimes the charge was listed as "murdering prisoners in violation of the laws of war" or similar language.

[85] In one case in which an accused was tried for both types of murder, the difference appears to be that simple murder applied to the killing of Filipino scouts and other officials in the employ of the United States (outside of ordinary combat), while the murder of civilians suspected to be spies was "in violation of the laws of war." *Id.* at 1249-50.

"[t]he killing of the deceased soldiers in an engagement with a regular detachment of the public enemy is not murder but a natural consequence incidental to a state of war."[86]

Similarly, defining as a war crime the "material support for terrorism"[87] does not appear to be supported by historical precedent. The military judge in the *Hamdan* military commission case deferred to Congress's determination in the MCA that "material support for terrorism" describes a traditional offense against the law of war, citing Civil War precedents for trying crimes such as cooperating with guerrillas or "guerrilla-marauders."[88] The Court of Military Commission Review affirmed,[89] but was overruled by the U.S. Court of Appeals for the D.C. Circuit.[90] The D.C. Circuit sitting *en banc* affirmed the conclusion that the material support offense is not a pre-existing war crime, nor one that is traditionally triable by military commission, and invalidated a conviction for it on ex post facto grounds, without deciding whether the Ex Post Facto Clause of the Constitution applies to foreigners held at Guantanamo or whether Congress could prospectively make material support a war crime for conduct committed after enactment of the MCA 2006.[91] The issue could potentially be headed to the Supreme Court.

The Supreme Court's decision in *Ex parte Milligan*[92] may have limited the extent to which such crimes may be tried by military commissions where martial law has not been established, and may also call into question whether such crimes are properly considered war crimes or should be treated as ordinary crimes triable by military commissions when necessity demands it.[93] Charges related to aiding guerrillas were typically accompanied by a specification stating that the accused was a citizen and owed allegiance to the United States, but not ordinarily stating that the activity

[86] *Id.* at 1362 (reprinting G.O. 171, July 13, 1901). It was also noted that the accused had not himself fired a weapon. The judge advocate went on to note that under the circumstances, conspiracy to commit the crime (murder, in violation of the laws of war) would not be warranted, either, but that the accused might have been found guilty of being a "war traitor" to the military government. In another case, a sentence for "murder" of a town official as well as "violations of the laws of war" for attacking a U.S. garrison was disapproved because "[t]he accused was a regularly commissioned officer of the hostile army engaged in a contemplated attack upon the enemy under the orders of his officers." *Id.* at 1231-32 (reprinting G.O., 197, July 27, 1901). That the participants had covered their uniforms and weapons during the operation was excused as a "ruse de guerre," and the killing of the official justified by his resistance to being taken prisoner. *Id.*

[87] 10 U.S.C. §950t(b)(25)(incorporating the definition found in 18 U.S.C. §2339A).

[88] United States v. Hamdan, Ruling on Motion to Dismiss (Ex Post Facto) D-012 (July 14, 2008), *available at* http://howappealing.law.com/HamdanRulingMotionsToDismissExPostFacto.pdf

[89] Hamdan v. United States, 801 F. Supp. 2d 1247 (USCMCR 2011).

[90] Hamdan v. United States, 696 F.3d 1238 (D.C. Cir. 2012); Al Bahlul v. United States, 2014 WL 3437485 (D.C. Cir. 2014)(en banc).

[91] Al Bahlul, 2014 WL 3437485.

[92] 71 U.S. (4 Wall.) 2 (1866). Lambdin Milligan and others were tried by military commission for conspiracy and "violations of the law of war," among other offenses, for participating in a secret armed organization opposed to the Union's efforts to prevent the secession of southern states and planning to use force in aid of the rebellion. G.O. 27, HQ District of Indiana (May 9, 1865), *reprinted in* [Series II], vol. 8 OFFICIAL RECORDS 543 - 49. The Supreme Court, while not disputing military commission jurisdiction over violations of the "laws and usages of war," stated those laws and usages "... can never be applied to citizens in states which have upheld the authority of the government, and where the courts are open and their process unobstructed." 71 U.S. at 121. By treating the case as one related to the legitimacy of martial law, the Court implicitly rejected the government's position that such activities, when committed by unprivileged belligerents, were amenable to military jurisdiction as violations of the law of war. *Compare id. with Ex parte* Quirin, 317 U.S. 1 (1941) (military commission jurisdiction appropriate for German saboteurs who breached U.S. coastal defenses despite absence of martial law).

[93] *See* cases listed *supra* note 83.

violated the law of war,[94] suggesting that the offense was a violation of martial law rather than the international law of war applicable to belligerents.

Many persons were tried by military commissions during the Philippine Insurrection for consorting with insurgents or other armed outlaws, but only after the commanding general issued a proclamation to the public explaining its obligation under the law of military occupation (a subset of the law of war analogous to martial law) to refrain from such activity.[95] The Obama Administration earlier expressed misgivings as to whether the crime of "material support for terrorism" amounts to an *ex post facto* law, and recommended the offense be eliminated from the MCA,[96] prior to attempting unsuccessfully to defend convictions for material support at the D.C. Circuit. All but one of the detainees against whom charges had been filed prior to 2011 had at least one count of "material support for terrorism" among them,[97] although in most cases the allegations underlying the charge appeared under other charges as well. Congress chose not to eliminate the material support charge when it amended the MCA in 2009. Newer cases have avoided the charge, although one case appears to charge equivalent conduct as "aiding the enemy" under UCMJ article 904.[98]

Temporal and Spatial Jurisdiction

The law of war has traditionally applied within the territorial and temporal boundaries of an armed conflict between at least two belligerents.[99] It traditionally has not been applied to conduct occurring on the territory of neutral states or on territory not under the control of a belligerent, to conduct that preceded the outbreak of hostilities, or to conduct during hostilities that do not amount to an armed conflict. Unlike the conflict in Afghanistan, the conflict related to the

[94] G.O. 4, HQ Dept. of the Missouri (January 16, 1864) 7 (accused was convicted and banished to Iowa on a charge of "harboring and feeding guerrillas"); G.O. 164, HQ, Dept. of the Missouri 8 (September 8, 1864) (conviction of "harboring and feeding guerrillas" as well as "giving aid and comfort to rebel enemies ... "); G.O. 236, HQ, Dept. of the Missouri 8 (December 26, 1864) ("harboring and feeding guerrillas").

[95] U.S. Congress, Senate Committee on the Philippines, *Affairs in the Philippine Islands*, 57th Cong., 1st sess., April 10, 1902, S.Hrg. 57-331 (Washington: GPO, 1902), pp. 1943-1946 (Statement explaining martial law and reprint of proclamation by Gen. Arthur McArthur of December 10, 1900). It appears that the terms "martial law" and the "law of hostile [or belligerent] occupation" were used interchangeably.

[96] U.S. Congress, Senate Committee on Armed Services, *Military Commissions*, 111th Cong., 1st sess., July 7, 2009 (Submitted statement of David Kris, Assistant Attorney General)("[T]here are serious questions as to whether material support for terrorism or terrorist groups is a traditional violation of the law of war. The President has made clear that military commissions are to be used only to prosecute law of war offenses. Although identifying traditional law of war offenses can be a difficult legal and historical exercise, our experts believe that there is a significant risk that appellate courts will ultimately conclude that material support for terrorism is not a traditional law of war offense, thereby reversing hard-won convictions and leading to questions about the system's legitimacy.")

[97] Mohammed Jawad was originally charged with attempted murder in violation of the law of war and attempt to cause serious bodily injury. Both charges were later dropped. Charge sheets are available at http://www.mc mil.

[98] Almed al Darbi was charged with aiding the enemy, among other offenses, in connection with terrorist attacks against shipping vessels. Abd al-Rahim Al-Nashiri is also charged with for offenses related to the bombing of the *USS Cole* in the Gulf of Aden and another attack on a vessel, but is not charged with aiding the enemy.

[99] *See* WINTHROP, *supra* footnote 31, at 773 (the law of war "prescribes the rights and obligations of belligerents, or ... define[s] the status and relations not only of enemies—whether or not in arms—but also of persons under military government or martial law and persons simply resident or being upon the theatre of war, and which authorizes their trial and punishment when offenders"); *id* at 836 (military commissions have valid jurisdiction only in theater of war or territory under martial law or military government).

September 11 attacks does not have clear boundaries in time or space,[100] nor is it entirely clear in all cases who the belligerents are.

The broad reach of President Bush's M.O. to encompass conduct and persons customarily subject to ordinary criminal law evoked criticism that the claimed jurisdiction of the military commissions exceeded the customary law of armed conflict, although DOD regulation purported to restate customary law.[101] The MCA provides jurisdiction to military commissions over covered offenses "when committed by an alien unprivileged enemy belligerent before, on, or after September 11, 2001."[102] Further, the MCA states that it codifies offenses "that have traditionally been triable by military commission" and establishes no "new crimes that did not exist before [its] enactment"; and that therefore it "does not preclude trial for offenses that occurred before the date of the enactment of this subchapter, as so amended."[103] Whether, in fact, the offenses were established under the law of war prior to the enactment of the MCA has already been the subject of two successful challenges by defendants.[104]

In enacting the MCA, Congress seems to have provided the necessary statutory definitions of criminal offenses to overcome previous objections with respect to subject matter jurisdiction of military commissions. However, questions may still arise with respect to the necessity for conduct to occur in the context of hostilities in order to be triable by military commission. In 2008, the military judge in the *Hamdan* case concluded that a nexus with hostilities was required, holding that a charge of "[m]embership in a conspiracy that planned and carried out the attacks of September 11th, 2001 will be deemed to be in violation of the law of war; membership in a conspiracy that planned or carried out other attacks long before that date and unrelated to hostilities will not."[105]

Composition and Powers

The MCA provides for a qualified military judge to preside over panels of at least 5 military officers, except in the cases in which the death penalty is sought, in which case panels are to consist of 12 members unless that number are not reasonably available, in which case the

[100] Some may argue that no war has a specific deadline and that all conflicts are in a sense indefinite. In traditional armed conflicts, however, it has been relatively easy to identify when hostilities have ended; for example, upon the surrender or annihilation of one party, an annexation of territory under dispute, an armistice or peace treaty, or when one party to the conflict unilaterally withdraws its forces. *See* GERHARD VON GLAHN, LAW AMONG NATIONS 722-730 (6th ed. 1992).

[101] *See* Leila Nadya Sadat, *Terrorism and the Rule of Law*, 3 WASH. U. GLOBAL STUD. L. REV. 135, 146 (2004) (noting possibly advantageous domestic aspects of treating terrorist attacks as war crimes, but identifying possible pitfalls of creating a new international legal regime).

[102] 10 U.S.C. §948d.

[103] 10 U.S.C. §950p(d).

[104] Hamdan v. United States (*Hamdan II*), 696 F.3d 1238 (D.C. Cir. 2012), *overruled in part by* Al Bahlul v. United States, 2014 WL 3437485 (D.C. Cir. July 14, 2014)(en banc). *Hamdan II* held that Congress did not intend to apply the offense of material support of terrorism retroactively and invalidated the accused's conviction on statutory grounds. *Al Bahlul* overturned the statutory interpretation holding in *Hamdan II*, finding that Congress did intend for the offense to apply retroactively. The court then invalidated a conviction for material support on constitutional grounds, albeit without deciding whether the constitutional protection against prosecution for *ex post facto* crimes applies to foreigners held at Guantanamo.

[105] United States v. Hamdan, Ruling on Motion to Dismiss (Res Judicata) (April 2, 2008).

minimum is 9 panel members.[106] Procedures for assigning military judges as well as the particulars regarding the duties they are to perform are left to the Secretary of Defense to prescribe, except that the military judge may not be permitted to consult with members of the panel outside of the presence of the accused and counsel except as prescribed in 10 U.S.C. Section 949d.[107] The military judge has the authority to decide matters related to the admissibility of evidence, including the treatment of classified information, but has no authority to compel the government to produce classified information.

The MCA empowers military commissions to maintain decorum during proceedings. Previously, under the DOD rules prior to enactment of the 2006 MCA, the presiding officer was authorized "to act upon any contempt or breach of Commission rules and procedures," including disciplining any individual who violates any "laws, rules, regulations, or other orders" applicable to the commission, as the presiding officer saw fit. Presumably this power was to include not only military and civilian attorneys but also any witnesses who had been summoned under order of the Secretary of Defense.[108] The MCA, 10 U.S.C. §950t, authorizes the military commissions to "punish for contempt any person who uses any menacing word, sign, or gesture in its presence, or who disturbs its proceedings by any riot or disorder." It is unclear whether this section is meant to expand the jurisdiction of military commissions to cover non-enemy unprivileged belligerent witnesses or civilian observers, but the M.M.C. expressly provides for jurisdiction over all persons, including civilians, and permits military judges to sentence those convicted with both fines and terms of confinement.[109] In the case of military commissions established under the UCMJ, there is statutory authority for military commissions to punish contempt with a fine of $100, confinement for up to 30 days, or both.[110] Although the MCA does not set limits on punishment for contempt, the M.M.C. 2012 limits confinement to 30 days and fines to $1000.[111]

The MCA provides that military commissions have the same power as a general court-martial to compel witnesses to appear in a manner "similar to that which courts of the United States having criminal jurisdiction may lawfully issue."[112] However, rather than providing that the trial counsel (prosecution) and the defense are to have equal opportunity to obtain witnesses and evidence, as is the case in general courts-martial, the MCA provides the defense a "reasonable opportunity" to obtain witnesses and evidence, in a manner comparable "to the opportunity available to a criminal defendant" in an article III court.[113] The M.M.C. provides the trial counsel with responsibility for producing witnesses requested by the defense, unless trial counsel determines the witness's

[106] 10 U.S.C. §949m.

[107] 10 U.S.C. §948j.

[108] *See* M.C.O. No. 1 §3(C) (asserting jurisdiction over participants in commission proceedings "as necessary to preserve the integrity and order of the proceedings").

[109] Rule for Military Commissions (R.M.C.) 809, M.M.C. 2012 *supra* footnote 71, at II-78.

[110] *See* 10 U.S.C. §848. This section is made inapplicable to military commissions in chapter 47A by MCA 2006 §4

[111] R.M.C. 809, M.M.C. 2012, *supra* footnote 71, at II-79.

[112] 10 U.S.C. §949j. P.L. 111-84 §1807 expresses the sense of Congress that

> (1) the fairness and effectiveness of the military commissions system under chapter 47A of title 10, United States Code (as amended by section 1802), will depend to a significant degree on the adequacy of defense counsel and associated resources for individuals accused, particularly in the case of capital cases, under such chapter 47A; and
>
> (2) defense counsel in military commission cases, particularly in capital cases, under such chapter 47A of title 10, United States Code (as so amended), should be fully resourced as provided in such chapter 47A.

[113] 10 U.S.C. §949j.

testimony is not required or is protected, but the defense counsel may appeal the determination to the convening authority or, after referral, the military judge.[114]

Under article 47 of the UCMJ, a duly subpoenaed witness who is not subject to the UCMJ and who refuses to appear before a military commission may be prosecuted in federal court.[115] Presumably, this article could be used to prosecute civilians residing in U.S. territory who refuse to comply with a subpoena issued under the MCA. The M.M.C. provides the military judge or any person designated to take evidence authority to issue a subpoena to compel the presence of a witness or the production of documents. As is the case with general courts-martial, the military judge may issue a warrant of attachment to compel the presence of a witness who refuses to comply with a subpoena.[116] Subpoena authority under the UCMJ may not be used to compel a civilian witness to travel abroad in order to provide testimony,[117] so the corresponding authority under the MCA may be insufficient to compel civilian witnesses to travel to Cuba. Testimony by video transmission may be permitted in such cases.[118]

One of the perceived shortcomings of President Bush's M.O. had to do with the problem of command influence over commission personnel. M.C.O. No. 1 provided for a "full and fair trial," but contained few specific safeguards to address the issue of impartiality. The President or his designee were empowered to decide which charges to press; to select the members of the panel, the prosecution and the defense counsel, and the members of the review panel; and to approve and implement the final outcome. The President or his designees had the authority to write procedural rules, interpret them, enforce them, and amend them. Justice Kennedy remarked in his concurring opinion in *Hamdan v. Rumsfed* that the concentration of authority in the Appointing Authority was a significant departure from the structural safeguards Congress has built into the military justice system.[119]

The MCA, by providing requirements for the procedural rules to guard against command influence, may alleviate some of these concerns. In particular, the MCA prohibits the unlawful influence of military commissions and provides that neither the military commission members nor military counsel may have adverse actions taken against them in performance reviews. Many of the procedural rules are left to the discretion of the Secretary of Defense or his designee, more so than is the case under the UCMJ. Rule 104 of the Rules for Military Commissions (R.M.C.) prohibits command influence in terms similar to those in the Manual for Courts-Martial, except that they apply more broadly to "all persons" rather than only to "all persons subject to the [UCMJ]."

On the other hand, it has been argued that the multiple roles assigned to the convening authority, that is, the DOD official who decides which charges to bring, allocates resources among the

---

114 R.M.C. 703.

115 *See* 10 U.S.C. §847. It is unclear how witnesses are "duly subpoenaed" for military commissions established under the UCMJ. 10 U.S.C. §846 empowers the president of a court-martial to compel witnesses to appear and testify and to compel production of evidence, but this statutory authority does not explicitly apply to military commissions. The subpoena power extends to "any part of the United States, or the Territories, Commonwealth and possessions."

116 R.M.C. 703; R.C.M. 703.

117 DAVID SCHLEUTER, MILITARY CRIMINAL JUSTICE: PRACTICE AND PROCEDURE §11-2(D)(2) (5th ed. 1999); United States v. Bennett, 12 M.J. 463 (C.M.A. 1982).

118 Mil. Comm. R. Evid. 611(d).

119 *Hamdan*, 647-51 (Kennedy, J. concurring).

parties, and then approves or disapproves the findings of the military commission, create an inherent risk of unfairness (or the perception of unfairness).[120] While the convening authority for courts-martial also plays multiple roles, these functions serve as commanders' tools for enforcing discipline among subordinates, a context that arguably differs in important ways from bringing criminal cases against alleged enemies.[121] Improper influence by the legal advisor to the convening authority has been alleged at a few military commission proceedings, prompting military judges to issue orders in some cases granting relief.[122] Executive branch control over who serves as military judges has also led to charges of unfairness.[123]

Procedures Accorded the Accused

The MCA lists a minimum set of rights to be afforded the accused in any trial, and provides the accused an opportunity to appeal adverse verdicts to the United States Court of Appeals for the District of Columbia Circuit, but only "with respect to the findings and sentence as approved by the convening authority and as affirmed or set aside as incorrect in law by the United States Court of Military Commission Review." The circuit court is empowered to take action "only with respect to matters of law, including the sufficiency of the evidence to support the verdict."[124] The MCA provides that the accused is to be informed of the charges as soon as practicable after the charges and specifications are referred for trial.[125] The accused is to be presumed innocent until determined to be guilty. The presumption of innocence and the right against self-incrimination are to result in an entered plea of "Not Guilty" if the accused refuses to enter a plea or enters a "Guilty" plea that is determined to be involuntary or ill informed.[126] The accused has the right not to testify at trial and to have the opportunity to present evidence and cross-examine witnesses for the prosecution.[127]

---

[120] Gregory S. McNeal, *Beyond Guantánamo, Obstacles and Options*, 103 NW. U. L. REV. COLLOQUY 29, 32 (2008) (blaming "conflicting statutory provisions" for perceived undue influence at military commissions under the MCA).

[121] *See id.* at 34; U.S. Congress, House Committee on the Judiciary, Subcommittee on the Constitution, Civil Rights, and Civil Liberties, *Proposals for Reform of the Military Commissions System*, 111th Cong., 1st Sess., July 30, 2009 (statement of Peter R. Masciola, USAFG, Chief Defense Counsel Office of Military Commissions-Defense Washington, DC).

[122] United States v. Hamdan, Ruling on Motion to Dismiss (Unlawful Influence) (D-026) (May 9, 2008) (Ordering substitute legal advisor be appointed for reviewing the case); United States v. Jawad, Ruling on Motion to Dismiss—Unlawful Influence (D-004) (August 14, 2008) (finding the Legal Advisor's public expression of support for the military commission process and alignment with the prosecution to have "compromised the objectivity necessary to dispassionately and fairly evaluate the evidence and prepare the post-trial recommendation," consequently disqualifying the legal advisor from carrying out post-trial responsibilities in the case); United States v. al Darbi, Ruling on Defense Motion to Dismiss (D-011) (October 2, 2008) (denying as moot request for relief, while noting activities of previous Legal Advisor may have compromised objectivity in necessary to fairly evaluate evidence and prepare post-trial recommendation).

[123] United States v. Khadr, Ruling on Defense Motion to Dismiss (D-076) (August 15, 2008) (denying relief where military judge was replaced after expiration of recall to active duty).

[124] 10 U.S.C. §950g. Previously, appeals could challenge only whether "the final decision was consistent with the standards and procedures specified" in the MCA, and "to the extent applicable, the Constitution and the laws of the United States."

[125] 10 U.S.C. §948q.

[126] 10 U.S.C. §949i.

[127] 10 U.S.C. §949a(b).

Open Hearing

Because the public, and not just the accused, has a constitutionally protected interest in public trials, the extent to which trials by military commission are open to the press and public may be subject to challenge by media representatives.[128] The First Amendment right of public access extends to trials by court-martial,[129] but is not absolute. It does not impose on the government a duty "to accord the press special access to information not shared by members of the public generally."[130] The reporters' right to gather information does not include an absolute right to gain access to areas not open to the public.[131] In general, trials may be closed only where the following test is met: the party seeking closure demonstrates an overriding interest that is likely to be prejudiced; the closure is narrowly tailored to protect that interest; the trial court has considered reasonable alternatives to closure; and the trial court makes adequate findings to support the closure.[132]

The MCA provides that the military commission judge may close portions of a trial only to protect information from disclosure where such disclosure could reasonably be expected to cause damage to the national security, such as information about intelligence or law enforcement sources, methods, or activities; or to ensure the physical safety of individuals.[133] The information to be protected from disclosure does not necessarily have to be classified. To the extent that the exclusion of the press and public is based on the discretion of the military judge without consideration of the constitutional requirements relative to the specific exigencies of the case at trial, the procedures may implicate the First Amendment rights of the press and public. The M.M.C. provides, in Rule 806, that the military judge may close proceedings only to protect information designated for such protection by a government agency or to secure the physical safety of individuals. However, the rule also provides that "in order to maintain the dignity and decorum of the proceedings or for other good cause, the military judge may reasonably limit the number of spectators in, and the means of access to, the courtroom, and exclude specific persons from the courtroom." Such limitations must be supported by written findings.

One method military judges have adopted to protect classified information without closing a hearing to the public is to employ a time-delay on the audio feed of the proceedings to the public in the gallery in order to permit the judge or other authorized person to turn off the audio in the event classified information has been or is about to be disclosed.[134] The measure was said to be necessary because the statements of the accused are presumptively classified. If the switch is

---

[128] *See* Globe Newspaper Co. v. Super. Ct., 457 U.S. 596, 602 (1982) (newspaper had standing to challenge court order closing portions of criminal trial). The Court of Appeals for the Armed Forces has ruled that it has no jurisdiction to hear a challenge by media representatives to closures in a court-martial case. Center for Constitutional Rights v. United States, 72 M.J. 126 (C.A.A.F. 2013).

[129] United States v. Hershey, 20 M.J. 433 (C.M.A.1985), *cert. denied*, 474 U.S. 1062 (1986); United States v. Grunden, 2 M.J. 116 (C.M.A.1977). The press has standing to challenge closure of military justice proceedings. ABC, Inc. v. Powell, 47 M.J. 363, 365 (1997).

[130] Pell v. Procunier, 417 U.S. 817, 822-24 (1974).

[131] *See* Juan R. Torruella, *On the Slippery Slopes of Afghanistan: Military Commissions and the Exercise of Presidential Power*, 4 U. PA. J. CONST. L. 648, 718 (2002) (noting that proceedings held at the Guantánamo Bay Naval Station may be *de facto* closed due to the physical isolation of the facility).

[132] *See* Press-Enterprise Co. v. Superior Court of California, 464 U.S. 501 (1984).

[133] 10 U.S.C. §949d(c).

[134] *E.g.*, United States v. Hamdan, Protective Order #3 (June 4, 2008).

activated, the judge was to order a halt to the proceedings to evaluate the nature of the information or to permit the prosecution to assert a national security privilege.

The MCA of 2009 inserted a new subtitle V to provide procedures for handling classified or sensitive information, including the closure of evidentiary hearings when such information is to be discussed, the sealing of records, and the issuance of protective orders. It states that the trial counsel may "object to any question or line of inquiry that may require the witness to disclose classified information not previously found to be admissible" during testimony.[135] In such circumstances, the military judge is to "take such suitable action to determine whether the response is admissible as will safeguard against the compromise of any classified information," which may leave room for the use of time delay devices as described above, though the measure isn't expressly authorized.

The American Civil Liberties Union (ACLU) and various media groups filed a petition for mandamus with the Court of Military Commission Review (CMCR)[136] challenging the scope of the protective order issued in the case against the five alleged September 11 conspirators on the basis of its perceived inconsistency with the First Amendment. The CMCR denied the writ without deciding whether it had jurisdiction to issue the writ, finding the controversy to be unripe for decision.[137]

Right to Be Present

Under UCMJ art. 39,[138] the accused at a court-martial has the right to be present at all proceedings other than the deliberation of the members. Under the DOD rules for military commissions prior to the MCA, the accused or the accused's civilian attorney could be precluded from attending portions of the trial for reasons involving national security, but a detailed (assigned) defense counsel was to be present for all hearings.[139] The MCA does not provide for the exclusion of the accused from portions of his trial, and does not allow classified information to be presented to panel members that is not disclosed to the accused. The accused may be excluded from trial proceedings (other than panel deliberations) by the military judge only upon a determination that the accused persists in disruptive or dangerous conduct.[140] However, the accused may be excluded from *in camera* considerations regarding the treatment of classified information.[141] The accused may not waive the right to be present at his trial, but may forfeit it through disruptive behavior or refusal to attend proceedings.[142]

---

[135] 10 U.S.C. §949p-7.

[136] For more information about the Court of Military Commission Review (CMCR), see *infra* at p. 31.

[137] ACLU v. United States, CMCR Case No. 13-003 (March 27, 2013), *available at* http://www mc mil/Portals/0/pdfs/ ACLU13-003/13-003%20ACLU%20Writ%20%28Ordering%20Dismissal%29%20%28J.%20Silliman%20Concur%29%20%28Mar%20 27%202013%29.pdf.

[138] 10 U.S.C. §839.

[139] That the accused could be excluded from portions of own trial and prevented from learning what evidence was introduced was among the factors that the *Hamdan* Court found most troubling about the military commissions established pursuant to President Bush's M.O. 548 U.S. at 614.

[140] 10 U.S.C. §949d(d).

[141] United States v. Khadr, Ruling on Defense Motion for Appropriate Relief (D-015) (February 21, 2008).

[142] R.M.C. 804 (discussion).

Right to Counsel

As is the case in military courts-martial, an accused before a military commission under the MCA has the right to have military counsel assigned free of charge. The right to counsel attaches much earlier in the regular military justice system, where the accused has a right to request an attorney prior to being interrogated about conduct relating to the charges contemplated, than under the MCA. Under the MCA, at least one qualifying military defense counsel is to be detailed "as soon as practicable."[143] The accused may also hire a civilian attorney who meets specific qualifications and agrees to comply with all applicable rules. If civilian counsel is hired, the detailed military counsel serves as associate counsel.[144] Unlike the previous DOD rules, the MCA provides that the accused has the right to self-representation.[145]

Previous DOD rules provided that defense counsel was to be assigned free of cost once charges were referred, but permitted the accused to request another Judge Advocate General (JAG) officer to be assigned as a replacement if available in accordance with any applicable instructions or supplementary regulations that might later be issued.[146] The MCA, as amended, incorporates this measure, providing the accused an opportunity to request a specific JAG officer to act as counsel, if the requested officer is reasonably available.[147] DOD regulations provide that the accused may request a specific military attorney from the defense team at the beginning of the proceedings, and may request a replacement counsel from the Chief Defense Counsel if he believes his detailed counsel has been ineffective or if he is otherwise materially dissatisfied with his assigned counsel.[148] The M.M.C. provides that, in the event the accused elects to represent himself, the detailed counsel shall serve as "standby counsel,"[149] and the military judge may require that such defense counsel remain present during proceedings.[150]

The MCA requires civilian attorneys defending an accused before military commission to meet the same strict qualifications that applied under DOD rules.[151] A civilian attorney must be a U.S. citizen with at least a SECRET clearance with membership in any state or territorial bar and no disciplinary record.[152] The MCA does not set forth in any detail what rules might be established to govern the conduct of civilian counsel. Under the last-issued regulation, the Chief Defense Counsel has the responsibility of determining the eligibility of civilian defense counsel, and may reconsider the determination based on "subsequently discovered information indicating material

---

143 10 U.S.C. §948k. The MCA 2006 required only that defense counsel be detailed "as soon as practicable after the swearing of charges against the accused."

144 10 U.S.C. §949c(b); R.M.C. 804.

145 10 U.S.C. §949a(b)(2)(D). The military judge can revoke the accused's right to self-representation if the accused fails to conduct his defense within the relevant rules and decorum applicable in military commission trials. Prior to the 2006 MCA, M.C.I. No. 4 required detailed defense counsel to "defend the accused zealously within the bounds of the law ... notwithstanding any intention expressed by the accused to represent himself." M.C.I. No. 4 §3(C).

146 M.C.O. No. 1 §4(C).

147 10 U.S.C. §949c(b)(2).

148 Regulation for Trial by Military Commissions, Para. 9-2. The accused may request a specific JAG officer from the cadre of officers assigned to the Defense Counsel's Office, but does not have a right to choose. R.C.M. 506 was amended to provide the accused an opportunity to choose military defense counsel from among military counsel assigned to the Office of Military Commissions as defense counsel.

149 R.M.C. 501.

150 R.M.C. 506(d).

151 10 U.S.C. §949c(b).

152 10 U.S.C. §949c, R.M.C. 502(d)(3).

nondisclosure or misrepresentation in the application, or material violation of obligations of the civilian defense counsel, or other good cause."[153] Alternatively, the Chief Defense Counsel may refer the matter to either the convening authority or the DOD Deputy General Counsel (Personnel and Health Policy), who may revoke or suspend the qualification of any member of the civilian defense counsel pool.

The MCA does not address the monitoring of communications between the accused and his attorney, and does not provide for an attorney-client privilege. Rule 502 of the Military Commission Rules of Evidence (Mil. Comm. R. Evid.) provides for substantially the same lawyer-client privilege that applies in courts-martial.[154] With respect to the monitoring of attorney-client communications, the previous DOD rules for military commissions initially provided that civilian counsel were required to agree that communications with the client were subject to monitoring. That requirement was later modified to require prior notification and to permit the attorney to notify the client when monitoring is to occur.[155] Although the government was not permitted to use information against the accused at trial, some argued that the absence of the normal attorney-client privilege could impede communications between them, possibly decreasing the effectiveness of counsel. Civilian attorneys were bound to inform the military counsel upon learning of information about a pending crime that could lead to "death, substantial bodily harm, or a significant impairment of national security."[156] The required agreement under the current regulations imposes a similar duty to inform, but does not mention monitoring of communications.[157] The revelation that the rooms where attorneys are permitted to meet with clients were fitted with hidden listening devices has caused some concern among defense attorneys at military commission proceedings.[158]

Evidentiary Matters

The Sixth Amendment to the U.S. Constitution guarantees that those accused in criminal prosecutions have the right to be "confronted with the witnesses against [them]" and to have "compulsory process for obtaining witnesses in [their] favor."[159] The Supreme Court has held that "[t]he central concern of the Confrontation Clause is to ensure the reliability of the evidence against a criminal defendant by subjecting it to rigorous testing in the context of an adversary

---

[153] Regulation for Trial by Military Commissions 2011, Para. 9-5(C).

[154] Mil. R. Evid. 502.

[155] *See* M.C.O. No. 3, "Special Administrative Measures for Certain Communications Subject to Monitoring." The required affidavit and agreement annexed to M.C.I. No. 3 was modified to eliminate the following language:

> I understand that my communications with my client, even if traditionally covered by the attorney-client privilege, may be subject to monitoring or review by government officials, using any available means, for security and intelligence purposes. I understand that any such monitoring will only take place in limited circumstances when approved by proper authority, and that any evidence or information derived from such communications will not be used in proceedings against the Accused who made or received the relevant communication.

[156] M.C.I. No. 5, Annex B §II(J).

[157] Regulation for Trial by Military Commissions 2011, Figure 9.2. Affidavit and Agreement by Civilian Defense Counsel, II(J).

[158] *See* Carol Rosenberg, *FBI hid microphones in Guantánamo, but no one listened, prison commander testifies,* MIAMI HERALD, February 13, 2013, *available at* http://www miamiherald.com/2013/02/13/3232992/fbi-hid-microphones-in-guantanamo html.

[159] U.S. CONST. Amdt. VI applies in courts-martial. *E.g.* United States v. Scheffer, 523 U.S. 303 (1998).

proceeding before the trier of fact."[160] In courts-martial, the Military Rules of Evidence (Mil. R. Evid.)[161] provide that "[a]ll relevant evidence is admissible, except as otherwise provided by the Constitution of the United States [and other applicable statutes, regulations and rules]."[162] Relevant evidence is excluded if its probative value is outweighed by other factors.[163] The accused has the right to view any documents in the possession of the prosecution related to the charges, and evidence that reasonably tends to negate the guilt of the accused, reduce the degree of guilt, or reduce the punishment,[164] with some allowance for protecting non-relevant classified information.[165]

Supporters of the use of military commissions to try suspected terrorists have viewed the possibility of employing evidentiary standards that vary from those used in federal courts or in military courts-martial as a significant advantage over those courts. The Supreme Court seemed to indicate that the previous DOD rules were inadequate under international law, remarking that "various provisions of Commission Order No. 1 dispense with the principles, articulated in Article 75 [of Protocol I to the Geneva Conventions] and indisputably part of the customary international law, that an accused must, absent disruptive conduct or consent, be present for his trial and must be privy to the evidence against him."[166]

The MCA provides that the accused has the right "to present evidence in [his] defense, to cross-examine the witnesses who testify against [him], and to examine and respond to evidence admitted against [him] on the issue of guilt or innocence and for sentencing."[167] It is not clear what evidence might be excluded from this requirement as irrelevant to the issues of guilt, innocence, or appropriate punishment. It is possible that this provision could be interpreted not to apply to evidence relevant to the credibility of a witness or the authenticity of a document, so that the accused would have no right to examine and respond to such evidence, unless expressly provided elsewhere in the MCA.

Discovery

The MCA provides that defense counsel is to be afforded a reasonable opportunity to obtain witnesses and other evidence, including evidence in the possession of the United States, as

---

160 Maryland v. Craig, 497 U.S. 836, 845 (1990).

161 The Military Rules of Evidence (Mil. R. Evid.) are contained in the Manual for Courts-Martial (M.C.M.), established as Exec. Order No. 12473, Manual for Courts-Martial, United States, 49 *Federal Register* 17,152, (April 23, 1984), as amended. The M.C.M. also contains the procedural rules for courts-martial, known as the Rules For Courts-Martial (R.C.M.).

162 Mil. R. Evid. 402.

163 Mil. R. Evid. 403 (relevant evidence may be excluded "if its probative value is substantially outweighed by the danger of unfair prejudice, confusion of the issues, or misleading the members, or by considerations of undue delay, waste of time, or needless presentation of cumulative evidence").

164 *See* R.C.M. 701(a)(6).

165 Mil. R. Evid. 505 provides procedures similar to the Classified Information Procedures Act (CIPA) that applies in civilian court.

166 Hamdan v. Rumsfeld, 548 U.S. 557, 635 (2006)(while accepting that the government "has a compelling interest in denying [the accused] access to certain sensitive information," stating that "at least absent express statutory provision to the contrary, information used to convict a person of a crime must be disclosed to him"). The Court viewed the international law of war to be incorporated by Congress into the UCMJ language authorizing military commissions.

167 10 U.S.C. §949a.

specified in regulations prescribed by the Secretary of Defense.[168] It does not guarantee the defense equal opportunity with the prosecution to obtain such evidence, as is the case at general courts-martial.[169] The MCA provides that all of the information admitted into evidence at trial under any rule must be provided to the accused.[170] The accused is also entitled to exculpatory and mitigating information known to the prosecution or investigators,[171] with procedures permitting some variance for security concerns.[172]

The MCA provides for the protection of national security information during the discovery phase of a trial under procedures similar to the Classified Information Procedures Act and the Manual for Courts-Martial.[173] Classified information is privileged and need not be disclosed.[174] Where M.C.O. No. 1 permitted the withholding of any "Protected Information,"[175] the MCA permits the government to withhold only information determined by the United States Government pursuant to statute, executive order, or regulation to require protection against unauthorized disclosure for reasons of national security.[176] Further, if the government wishes to withhold any classified information, the trial counsel must submit a declaration, signed by a knowledgeable official with classification authority, invoking the United States' classified information privilege and setting forth the damage to the national security that the discovery of or access to such information reasonably could be expected to cause.[177] The military judge may authorize production of the classified information if she determines that it would be "noncumulative, relevant, and helpful to a legally cognizable defense, rebuttal of the prosecution's case, or to sentencing," in accordance with standards generally applicable in federal criminal cases.[178] Specifically, the military judge may authorize the government to delete specified portions of evidence to be made available to the accused, or may allow an unclassified summary or statement setting forth the facts the evidence would tend to prove, to the extent practicable in accordance with the rules used at general courts-martial.[179] Trial counsel may submit applications for protective measures on an ex parte basis, and the MCA does not provide defense counsel with access to the classified information that serves as the basis for substitute or redacted proffers. The decision to permit a substitution or grant other relief, which is required so long as the military judge determines such relief would "provide the accused with substantially the same ability to make a defense" as would access to the classified

---

[168] 10 U.S.C. §949j.

[169] 10 U.S.C. §846.

[170] 10 U.S.C. §949p-1(b).

[171] 10 U.S.C. §949j. The prosecution is obligated to provide, as soon as practicable, information that is known or reasonably should be known to the prosecution or any government officials who participated in the investigation that tends to negate or mitigate the guilt of the accused of an offense charged or to impeach the credibility of a witness whom the government intends to call at trial. As soon as practicable after a finding of guilt, the prosecution is required to disclose any other information that might reasonably be viewed as mitigating factors for sentencing.

[172] 10 U.S.C. §§949p-(1-7). Where potential evidence is classified, trial counsel is to work with the original classification authority to declassify the information to the maximum extent possible, but decisions not to declassify are not subject to review by the military judge. 10 U.S.C. §949p-1(c).

[173] 10 U.S.C. §949p-4.

[174] 10 U.S.C. §949p-1(a).

[175] M.C.O. No. 1, §6 (defining "Protected Information" to include classified or classifiable information, information protected "by law or rule from unauthorized disclosure," information that could endanger trial participants, intelligence and law enforcement sources, methods or activities, or "information concerning other national security interests").

[176] 10 U.S.C. §§948a(2) & 949p-1.

[177] 10 U.S.C. §949p-4(a).

[178] *Id.*

[179] 10 U.S.C. §949p-4(b).

information itself, is not subject to a motion for reconsideration, but all of the submitted information and hearing transcripts are sealed and preserved for submission in case of appeal.

Admissibility of Evidence

The Secretary of Defense may prescribe in the rules of evidence that evidence is admissible as authentic if the military judge determines that "there is sufficient evidence that the evidence is what it is claimed to be," and instructs the members that they may consider any issue as to authentication or identification of evidence in determining the weight, if any, to be given to the evidence.[180] The accused is entitled to the exclusion of evidence that is not probative or reliable, or of evidence the probative value of which is substantially outweighed by the "danger of unfair prejudice, confusion of the issues, or misleading the members"; or by "considerations of undue delay, waste of time, or needless presentation of cumulative evidence."[181]

Coerced Statements

The MCA prohibits the use of statements obtained through torture as evidence in a trial, except to prove torture where the defendant is accused of committing torture. For information obtained through coercion that does not amount to torture, the MCA 2006 provided a different standard for admissibility depending on whether the statement was obtained prior to or after the enactment of the DTA. Statements elicited through such methods prior to the DTA were admissible if the military judge were to find that the "totality of circumstances under which the statement was made renders it reliable and possessing sufficient probative value" and "the interests of justice would best be served" by admission of the statement.[182] Statements taken after passage of the DTA were admissible if, in addition to the two criteria above, the military judge were to find that "the interrogation methods used to obtain the statement do not violate the cruel, inhuman, or degrading treatment prohibited by section 1003 of the Detainee Treatment Act."[183]

The MCA 2009 eliminates the distinction above, making statements obtained through cruel, inhuman or degrading methods inadmissible regardless of when they were made.[184] The Obama Administration had already amended the military commission regulations in May 2009 to remove the discrepancy.[185] Otherwise, out-of-court statements by the accused may be admitted if the military judge finds that the totality of the circumstances renders the statement reliable and

[180] 10 U.S.C. §949a(b)(C)(3). Under the military commissions established by the MCA2006, evidence was admissible if the commission deemed it to have "probative value to a reasonable person." Previous 10 U.S.C. §949a(b)(2)(a). This standard was met if "a reasonable person would regard the evidence as making the existence of any fact that is of consequence to a determination of the commission action more probable or less probable than it would be without the evidence." Mil. Comm. R. Evid. 401. At courts-martial, evidence is admitted if it is "relevant," meaning "tending to make the existence of any fact that is of consequence to the determination of the action more probable or less probable than it would be without the evidence." Mil. R. Evid. 401. The elimination of the "probative value to a reasonable person" standard by the MCA 2009 did not result in any changes to Mil. Comm. R. Evid. 401. ("Probative" differs from "relevant" in that relevance includes an element of materiality to an issue, where "probative" simply means "tends to prove" a fact, whether or not the fact is material to the case).

[181] 10 U.S.C. §949a(b)(2)(F). Under the MCA2006, this right could be (and was) included in the procedural rules at the discretion of the Secretary of Defense.

[182] Previous 10 U.S.C. §948r(c).

[183] Previous 10 U.S.C. §948r(d).

[184] 10 U.S.C. §948r.

[185] Gates letter, *supra* footnote 20. *See* Mil. Comm. R. Evid. 304 (2012).

possessing sufficient probative value; and either that the statement was voluntarily given or that the statement was made "incident to lawful conduct during military operations at the point of capture or during closely related active combat engagement, and the interests of justice would best be served by admission of the statement into evidence."[186] Voluntariness is to be determined considering the totality of the circumstances, including the following:

> (1) The details of the taking of the statement, accounting for the circumstances of the conduct of military and intelligence operations during hostilities.
>
> (2) The characteristics of the accused, such as military training, age, and education level.
>
> (3) The lapse of time, change of place, or change in identity of the questioners between the statement sought to be admitted and any prior questioning of the accused.[187]

The defense is required to make any objections to the proposed use of any statements by the accused prior to entering a plea, if the trial counsel has disclosed the intent to use the statement, otherwise the objection will be deemed to have been waived.[188] The military judge may require the defense to establish the grounds for excluding the statement. However, the government has the burden of establishing the admissibility of the evidence. If the statement is ruled admissible, the defense is permitted to present evidence with respect to the voluntariness of the statement, and the military judge must instruct the members to consider that factor in according weight to the evidence. Testimony given by the accused for the purpose of denying having made a statement or for disputing the admissibility of a statement is not to be used against him for any purpose other than in prosecution for perjury or false statements.[189]

The current version of Mil. Comm. R. Evid. 304 is modeled on Mil. R. Evid. 304, which prescribes rules for courts-martial to provide for the admission into evidence of confessions and admissions (self-incriminating statements not amounting to an admission of guilt). Under court-martial rules, such a statement and any evidence derived as a result of such a statement are admissible only if the statement was made voluntarily. Involuntary statements are those elicited through coercion or other means in violation of constitutional due process. To be used as evidence of guilt against the accused at court martial, a confession or admission must be corroborated by independent evidence. There is no requirement for corroboration of such statements at military commissions; however, the military judge may take the existence of corroborating evidence into consideration in determining the probative value and reliability of the statement.

In one case before a military commission, the military judge ordered a detainee's statements to Afghan officials at the time of his capture suppressed on the basis of death threats against the detainee as well as his family.[190] Such treatment is regarded as torture under the Military Commission Rules of Evidence.[191] Further, the military judge ruled that statements subsequently made by the accused to U.S. interrogators likewise were required to be suppressed because they

[186] 10 U.S.C. §948r(c).

[187] 10 U.S.C. §948r(d).

[188] Mil. Comm. R. Evid. 304(d).

[189] Mil. Comm. R. Evid. 304(f).

[190] United States v. Jawad, ruling on Defense Motion to Suppress Out-of-Court Statements of the Accused to Afghan Authorities (D-022) (October 28, 2008).

[191] Mil. R. Evid. 304.

were taken under circumstances that did not sufficiently dissipate the coercive effect of the earlier threats.[192] The government sought to appeal the latter ruling, but later dropped the charges against the detainee after he prevailed in his habeas petition.[193]

Hearsay

Hearsay evidence is an out-of-court statement, whether oral, written, or conveyed through non-verbal conduct, introduced into evidence to prove the truth of the matter asserted. M.C.O. No. 1 did not exclude hearsay evidence. The MCA allows for the admission of hearsay evidence that would not be permitted under the Manual for Courts-Martial[194] only if the proponent of the evidence notifies the adverse party sufficiently in advance of trial of the intention to offer the evidence, as well as the "particulars of the evidence (including [unclassified] information on the general circumstances under which the evidence was obtained)."[195] Originally, the evidence was to be inadmissible only if the party opposing its admission "clearly demonstrates that the evidence is unreliable or lacking in probative value."[196] The May 2009 changes to the regulations reverse the burden of demonstrating reliability to the proponent of the evidence,[197] and the MCA 2009 reflects the change.

The rules regarding hearsay are provided in Mil. Comm. R. Evid. 801 to 807. In contrast to the relatively restrictive rule applied in courts-martial, where hearsay is not admissible except as permitted by a lengthy set of exceptions,[198] the military commission rules provide that hearsay *is* admissible on the same basis as any other form of evidence except as provided by these rules or an act of Congress, perhaps creating a presumption of admissibility for hearsay evidence in military commissions. Mil. Comm. R. Evid. 803 provides that hearsay may be admitted if it would be admissible under the rules applicable at courts-martial. Otherwise, hearsay is admissible only if the party proffering it notifies the adverse party with sufficient time in advance of trial or hearing of its intent to offer such evidence and provides any materials in its possession regarding the time, place, and conditions under which the statement was procured; and the military judge finds, considering the relevant circumstances,[199] that

> (A) the statement is offered as evidence of a material fact;
>
> (B) the statement is probative for which it is offered;

---

[192] United States v. Jawad, ruling on Defense Motion to Suppress Out-of-Court Statements of the Accused Made While in U.S. Custody (D-021) (November 19, 2008).

[193] For a detailed history of the Jawad case, see David J. R. Frakt, *Mohammed Jawad and the Military Commissions of Guantánamo*, 60 DUKE L.J. 1367 (2011).

[194] Mil. R. Evid. 801-807 provide procedures for determining the admissibility of hearsay evidence in courts-martial.

[195] 10 U.S.C. §949a(b)(3)(D).

[196] Previous 10 U.S.C. §949a(b)(2)(E) (rules that may be prescribed by the Secretary of Defense).

[197] Gates letter, *supra* footnote 20.

[198] Mil. R. Evid. 803 (exceptions for which the availability of the declarant is immaterial); Mil. R. Evid. 804 (exceptions applicable when declarant is unavailable); Mil. R. Evid. 807 (residual exception, which permits all other hearsay not covered by express exceptions when there are "equivalent circumstantial guarantees of trustworthiness" and the military judge determines the statement relates to a material fact, is more probative to that fact than other reasonably obtainable evidence, and that its introduction into evidence "serves the general purposes of the rules and the interest of justice").

[199] These circumstances include "the degree to which the statement is corroborated, the indicia of reliability within the statement itself, and whether the will of the declarant was overborne.... " Mil. Comm. R. Evid. 803(b)(2).

> (C) direct testimony from the witness is not available as a practical matter, taking into consideration the physical location of the witness, the unique circumstances of military and intelligence operations during hostilities, and the adverse impacts on military or intelligence operations that would likely result from the production of the witnesses; and
>
> (D) the general purposes of the rules of evidence and the interests of justice will best be served by admission of the statement into evidence.[200]

Under the previous rules, hearsay evidence was inadmissible if the opponent demonstrated by a preponderance of the evidence that such hearsay was unreliable under the totality of the circumstances.[201] The current rules do not expressly allocate the burden of proof as to reliability of hearsay evidence. Presumably it falls on the proponent of the evidence.

Classified Evidence

The MCA 2009 adopted rules for the protection of classified information that are similar to the Classified Information Procedures Act (CIPA),[202] which supplies rules for criminal trials in federal civilian courts. The rules in subchapter V of the MCA also adopt modifications to CIPA that reflect experience in courts that have construed it for use in federal terrorism trials.[203] The MCA directs military judges to view CIPA case law as authoritative unless such a construction would be inconsistent with provisions of the MCA.[204]

At military commissions convened pursuant to the MCA, classified information[205] is to be protected during all stages of proceedings and is privileged from disclosure for national security purposes.[206] Whenever the United States seeks to protect certain information from disclosure in any military commission case, the prosecution is to submit a declaration, signed by a knowledgeable official with classification authority, invoking the privilege and setting forth the damage to national security that would be expected to occur without protective measures.[207] The military judge may not authorize the discovery of or access to such information unless he determines that it would be relevant and useful to any part of the defense's case.[208] The military judge may authorize the United States to delete or withhold specified items of classified information from documents made available to the accused; substitute a summary of the information; or substitute a statement admitting relevant facts that the classified information would tend to prove.[209] The military judge must consider a claim of privilege and review any

---

[200] Mil. Comm. R. Evid. 803(b)(2). The language is identical to the MCA language found in 10 U.S.C. §949a(3)(D).

[201] Mil. Comm. R. Evid. 803(c) (2007 MCM).

[202] P.L. 96-456, October 15, 1980, codified at 18 U.S.C. App.

[203] *See* DAVID S. KRIS & J. DOUGLAS WILSON, 2 NATIONAL SECURITY INVESTIGATIONS & PROSECUTIONS 2D, §24:14 (2012).

[204] 10 U.S.C. §949p-1(d).

[205] Defined in 10 U.S.C. §948a(2) as "[a]ny information or material that has been determined by the United States Government pursuant to statute, Executive order, or regulation to require protection against unauthorized disclosure for reasons of national security" and "restricted data, as that term is defined in section 11y of the Atomic Energy Act of 1954 (42 U.S.C. 2014(y))."

[206] 10 U.S.C. §949p-1.

[207] 10 U.S.C. §949p-4.

[208] 10 U.S.C. §949p-4(a)(2).

[209] 10 U.S.C. §949p-4(b).

supporting materials in camera if requested by the government, and must grant the relief sought if he finds that the summary, statement, or other substitute would "provide the accused with substantially the same ability to make a defense as would discovery or access to the specific classified information."[210] The accused may not move for reconsideration of protective measures granted to the government if the order was entered pursuant to an ex parte showing.[211] The government, however, can bring an interlocutory appeal in the event the judge orders that classified information must be disclosed or imposes sanctions for the government's refusal to permit disclosure, or refuses a protective order sought by the government.[212]

With respect to the protection of intelligence sources and methods relevant to specific evidence, the military judge is required to permit trial counsel to introduce otherwise admissible evidence before the military commission without disclosing the "sources, methods, or activities by which the United States acquired the evidence" if the military judge finds that such information is otherwise admissible as evidence, that it is reliable, and that the redaction is consistent with affording the accused a fair trial.[213]

The MCA does not explicitly provide an opportunity for the accused to contest the admissibility of substitute evidence proffered under the above procedures. It does not appear to permit the accused or his counsel to examine the evidence or a proffered substitute prior to its presentation to the military commission. If constitutional standards required in the Sixth Amendment are held to apply to military commissions, the MCA may be open to challenge for affording the accused an insufficient opportunity to contest evidence.

Classified evidence is privileged under Mil. Comm. R. Evid. 505. During the examination of witnesses at trial, the trial counsel may make an objection to any question or motion that might lead to the disclosure of classified information.[214] The military judge is required to take appropriate action, such as taking a proffer of the nature of the information the witness might be expected to provide, reviewing the matter in camera if requested by the government. The judge may order that only parts of documents or other materials be entered into evidence, unless fairness dictates the whole ought to be considered.[215] In the event the defense reasonably expects to disclose classified information at trial, defense counsel must notify the trial counsel and the judge, and is precluded from disclosing information known or believed to be classified until the government has had a reasonable opportunity to move for an in camera determination as to protective measures.[216] In the event the military judge denies a government motion to provide a substitution or alternative to disclosures and the accused is prevented from disclosing classified information at trial due to the government's objection, the military judge may dismiss the case or, if the interest of justice is not served by dismissal, the judge may order other relief, such as dismissal of specified charges or specifications, finding against the government on any issue to

[210] 10 U.S.C. §949p-4(b)(3).

[211] 10 U.S.C. §949p-4(c).

[212] 10 U.S.C. §950d.

[213] 10 U.S.C. §949p-6(c).

[214] Mil. Comm. R. Evid. 505(i)(3).

[215] Mil. Comm. R. Evid. 505(i). Similar procedures are permitted in courts-martial. Mil. R. Evid. 505(j).

[216] Mil. Comm. R. Evid. 505(g). This rule is virtually identical to Mil. R. Evid. 505(h).

which the excluded evidence is relevant, or striking or precluding all or part of a witness's testimony.[217]

Sentencing

The MCA provides that military commissions may adjudge "any punishment not forbidden by [the MCA], including the penalty of death...."[218] It specifically proscribes punishment "by flogging, or by branding, marking, or tattooing on the body, or any other cruel or unusual punishment, ... or [by the] use of irons, single or double."[219] A vote of two-thirds of the members present is required for sentences of up to 10 years.[220] Longer sentences require the concurrence of three-fourths of the members present.[221] The death penalty must be approved unanimously, both as to guilt (except in the case of a guilty plea) and to the sentence, by all members present for the vote.[222]

In cases where the death penalty is sought, a panel of 12 members is required (unless the convening authority certifies that 12 members are not "reasonably available" because of physical conditions or military exigencies, in which case no fewer than nine are required), with all members present for the vote agreeing on the sentence. The death penalty must be expressly authorized for the offense,[223] and the charges referred to the commission must have expressly sought the penalty of death.[224] The death sentence may not be executed until the commission proceedings have been finally adjudged lawful and all appeals are exhausted,[225] and after the President approves the sentence.[226] The President is permitted to "commute, remit, or suspend [a death] sentence, or any part thereof, as he sees fit."[227] For sentences other than death, the Secretary of the Defense or the convening authority is permitted to adjust the sentence downward.[228]

Chapter X of the Rules for Military Commissions covers sentencing. "Aggravating factors" that may be presented by the trial counsel include evidence that "any offense of which the accused has been convicted comprises a violation of the law of war."[229] Unlike the rules for courts-martial, there is no express opportunity for the trial counsel to present evidence regarding rehabilitative

---

[217] Mil. Comm. R. Evid. 505(h). Similar sanctions may be applied at courts-martial. Mil. R. Evid. 505(i)(4)(E).

[218] 10 U.S.C. §948d.

[219] 10 U.S.C. §949s.

[220] 10 U.S.C. §949m.

[221] 10 U.S.C. §949m(b)(3).

[222] 10 U.S.C. §949m(b)(2).

[223] The death penalty may be authorized under the MCA, the UCMJ, or the laws of war. 10 U.S.C. §949m(b)(2). The MCA permits the death penalty for convictions of murder of a protected person or murder in violation of the law of war, or spying; and if death results, any of the following crimes: attacking civilians, taking hostages, employing poison or similar weapon, using protected persons as a shield, torture or cruel or inhuman treatment, intentionally causing serious bodily injury, maiming, using treachery or perfidy, hijacking or hazarding a vessel or aircraft, terrorism, and conspiracy to commit any of the crimes enumerated in 10 U.S.C. §950t.

[224] 10 U.S.C. §949m.

[225] An accused sentenced to death may neither waive his right to appeal nor withdraw an appeal. 10 U.S.C. §950c.

[226] 10 U.S.C. §950i(b)-(c).

[227] 10 U.S.C. §950i(b).

[228] 10 U.S.C. §950i(d).

[229] R.M.C. 1001(b)(2).

potential of the accused. However, the rules provide that the accused may make a sworn or unsworn statement to present mitigating or extenuating circumstances or to rebut evidence of aggravation submitted by the trial counsel. In the case of an unsworn statement, which may be written or oral, the accused is not subject to cross-examination by the trial counsel.[230]

The death penalty may only be adjudged if expressly authorized for the offense listed or if it is authorized under the law of war; and all 12 members of the commission voted to convict the accused (except in the case of a guilty plea);[231] found that at least one of the listed aggravating factors exists; agreed that such factors outweigh any extenuating or mitigating circumstances; and voted to impose the death penalty. Aggravating factors include that the offense resulted in the death of or substantially endangered the life of one or more other persons, the offense was committed for the purpose of receiving money or a thing of value, the offense involved torture or certain other mistreatment, the accused was also found guilty of another capital crime, the victim was below the age of 15, or that the victim was a protected person.[232] Other aggravating circumstances include specific law-of-war violations, which are not to be applied to offenses of which they are already an element.

Post-Trial Procedure

Subchapter VI of the MCA prescribes post-trial procedure and appeals, similar to procedures DOD had implemented. It provides for an administrative review of the trial record by the convening authority followed by a review panel. The MCA 2009 did not make major changes to the appellate structure.

Review and Appeal

The MCA 2006 codified the establishment of the review body set up under the pre-2006 DOD rules for military commissions.[233] The Court of Military Commission Review (CMCR) is composed of judges who meet the same qualifications as military judges or comparable qualifications for civilian judges.[234] The accused may appeal a final decision of the military commission with respect to issues of law to the CMCR. Like the UCMJ, the MCA prohibits the invalidation of a verdict or sentence due to an error of law unless the error materially prejudices the substantial rights of the accused.[235] If the CMCR approves the verdict, the accused may

[230] R.M.C. 1001(c)(2)(C). The trial counsel may rebut the statement. This procedure does not appear to differ substantially from that used in courts-martial.

[231] 10 U.S.C. §949m was modified to permit accused in capital cases to plead guilty, an option that is not available under the UCMJ. P.L. 112-81, §1030(a).

[232] R.M.C. 1004(c). Previous versions of the Manual included as an aggravating offense that "the accused was convicted of an offense, referred as capital, that is a violation of the law of war."

[233] M.C.I. No. 9 §4(C).

[234] 10 U.S.C. §950f. This section was modified in 2011 to remove an ambiguous reference to the judges on the court as "appellate military judges," which it was argued meant that judges had to be current appellate military judges and were disqualified once they were no longer actively serving on an appellate military court under the UCMJ. P.L. 112-81, §1034(c). It appears that judges appointed to the CMCR by the Secretary of Defense are still required to be appellate military judges at the time of appointment. There is no such requirement for those appointed by the President with the advice and consent of the Senate.

[235] 10 U.S.C. §859; 10 U.S.C. §950a(a).

appeal the final decision to the U.S. Court of Appeals for the District of Columbia Circuit.[236] Appellate court decisions may be reviewed by the Supreme Court under writ of certiorari.[237]

Post-trial procedures for military commissions are set forth in Chapter XI of the Rules for Military Commissions. Post-trial proceedings may be conducted to correct errors, omissions, or inconsistencies, where the revision can be accomplished without material prejudice to the accused.[238] Sessions without members may be ordered to reconsider any trial ruling that substantially affects the legal sufficiency of any findings of guilt or the sentence.[239]

Once the record is authenticated and forwarded to the convening authority, the accused is permitted, within 20 days unless additional time is approved, to submit matters relevant to whether to approve the sentence or disapprove findings of guilt.[240] The convening authority is required to consider written submissions. If the military commission has made a finding of guilty, the legal advisor also reviews the record and provides recommendations to the convening authority.[241] The convening authority may not take an action disapproving a finding of not guilty or a ruling that amounts to a finding of not guilty.[242] However, in the case of a finding of not guilty by reason of lack of mental responsibility, the convening authority may commit the accused to a suitable facility for treatment pending a hearing to determine whether the accused may be released or detained under less than the most stringent circumstances without posing a danger to others.[243]

Rehearings of guilty findings may be ordered at the discretion of the convening authority, except where there is a lack of sufficient evidence to support the charge or lesser included offense. Rehearings are permitted if evidence that should not have been admitted can be replaced by an admissible substitute.[244] Any part of a sentence served pursuant to the military commission's original holding counts toward any sentence that results from a hearing for resentencing.[245]

In all cases in which the convening authority approves a finding of guilty, the record is forwarded to the CMCR, unless the accused (where the sentence does not include death) waives review.[246] No relief may be granted by the CMCR unless an error of law prejudiced a substantial trial right

[236] 10 U.S.C. §950g. No collateral attack on the military commission's jurisdiction or verdict was permitted under the MCA 2006. 10 U.S.C. §949j(b) previously provided that

> Except as otherwise provided in this chapter and notwithstanding any other provision of law (including section 2241 of title 28 or any other habeas corpus provision), no court, justice, or judge shall have jurisdiction to hear or consider any claim or cause of action whatsoever, including any action pending on or filed after the date of the enactment of the Military Commissions Act of 2006, relating to the prosecution, trial, or judgment of a military commission under this chapter, including challenges to the lawfulness of procedures of military commissions under this chapter.

[237] 10 U.S.C. §950g.

[238] R.M.C. 1102(b).

[239] *Id.*

[240] R.M.C. 1105.

[241] R.M.C. 1106.

[242] R.M.C. 1107.

[243] R.M.C. 1107; R.M.C. 1102A.

[244] R.M.C. 1107(e).

[245] R.M.C. 1107(f)(5).

[246] R.M.C. 1111. Courts-martial findings are first forwarded to the Judge Advocate General of the particular service for legal review, R.C.M. 1112.

of the accused.[247] The accused has 20 days after receiving notification of the CMCR decision to submit a petition for review with the U.S. Court of Appeals for the District of Columbia Circuit. Within two years after a military commission conviction becomes final, an accused may petition the convening authority for a new trial on the ground of newly discovered evidence or fraud on the military commission.[248]

Protection Against Double Jeopardy

Prior to the MCA, DOD regulations for military commissions provided that the accused could not be tried for the same charge twice by any military commission once the commission's finding on that charge became final (meaning once the verdict and sentence had been approved).[249] However, the regulations appeared to permit revisions of a verdict prior to its becoming final in ways that might have resulted in double jeopardy.[250]

The MCA provides that "[n]o person may, without the person's consent, be tried by a military commission under this chapter a second time for the same offense."[251] Jeopardy attaches when a guilty finding becomes final after review of the case has been fully completed.[252] The MCA prevents double jeopardy in such cases by expressly eliminating the possibility that a finding that amounts to a verdict of not guilty is subject to reversal by the convening authority or to review by the CMCR or the D.C. Circuit. The severity of a sentence adjudged by the military commission cannot be increased on rehearing unless the sentence prescribed for the offense is mandatory.[253] These protections are covered in Chapter XI of the Rules for Military Commission. Proceedings are not authorized to reconsider any ruling that amounts to a finding of not guilty as to any charge or specification, except with respect to a charge where the record indicates guilt as to a specification that may be charged as a separate offense under the MCA.[254] Proceedings for increasing the severity of a sentence are not permitted unless the commission failed to adjudge a proper sentence under the MCA.[255]

The inadequacy of an indictment in specifying charges could raise double jeopardy concerns. If the charge does not adequately describe the offense, another trial for the same offense under a new description is not as easily prevented. The MCA requires that charges and specifications be signed under oath by a person with personal knowledge or reason to believe that matters set forth therein are true,[256] and requires that they be served on the accused written in a language he

[247] R.M.C. 1201.

[248] R.M.C. 1210. This option is not available to those convicted pursuant to a guilty plea.

[249] M.C.O. No. 1 §5(P). The finding was to become final when "the President or, if designated by the President, the Secretary of Defense makes a final decision thereon pursuant to Section 4(c)(8) of the President's Military Order and in accordance with Section 6(H)(6) of [M.C.O. No. 1]." *Id.* §6(H)(2).

[250] *See* CRS Report RL33688, *The Military Commissions Act of 2006: Analysis of Procedural Rules and Comparison with Previous DOD Rules and the Uniform Code of Military Justice.*

[251] 10 U.S.C. §949h.

[252] 10 U.S.C. §949h.

[253] 10 U.S.C. §950b(d)(2)(B).

[254] R.M.C. 1102(c).

[255] *Id.* R.M.C. 1102(c) of the 2007 M.M.C. also permitted rehearing where the sentence was less than that agreed to in a plea agreement.

[256] 10 U.S.C. §948q.

understands.[257] There is no express requirement regarding the specificity of the charges in the MCA, but the Rules for Military Commission provide that the charge must state the punitive article of the act, law of war, or offense as defined in the Manual for Military Commissions that the accused is alleged to have violated.[258] A specification must allege every element of the charged offense expressly or by necessary implication.[259] The Rules for Military Commissions make the trial counsel responsible for causing the accused to be served a copy of the charges in English and another language that the accused understands, where appropriate.[260] After the accused is arraigned, the military judge may permit minor changes in the charges and specifications before findings are announced if no substantial right of the accused is prejudiced, but no major changes may be made over the objection of the accused without a new referral.[261]

President Bush's 2001 Military Order also left open the possibility that a person subject to the order might be transferred at any time to some other governmental authority for trial, or that a person already charged for crimes in federal courts could be made subject to the Order and transferred for trial by military commission.[262] Double jeopardy might have arisen in either event, depending on whether jeopardy had attached prior to transfer, even if the trial did not result in a final verdict.[263] The MCA does not expressly address such transfers or prohibit trial in another forum. The Rules for Military Commissions, however, provide the accused a waivable right to move to dismiss charges on the basis that he has previously been tried by a federal civilian court for the same offense.[264]

The following charts provide a comparison of general courts-martial to the military tribunals under the Military Commissions Act of 2006 as initially enacted and as amended by the Military Commissions Act of 2009. **Chart 1** compares the legal authorities for establishing military tribunals (including courts-martial), the jurisdiction over persons and offenses, and the structures of the tribunals. **Chart 2**, which compares procedural safeguards, follows the same order and format used in CRS Report RL31262, *Selected Procedural Safeguards in Federal, Military, and International Courts*, by Jennifer K. Elsea, in order to facilitate comparison of the proposed legislation to safeguards provided in federal court,[265] the international military tribunals that tried World War II crimes at Nuremberg and Tokyo, and contemporary ad hoc tribunals set up by the UN Security Council to try crimes associated with hostilities in the former Yugoslavia and Rwanda.

---

[257] 10 U.S.C. §948s.

[258] R.M.C. 307.

[259] *Id.*

[260] R.M.C. 602.

[261] R.M.C. 603.

[262] M.O. §7(e).

[263] The MCA does not define when jeopardy attaches in the event a trial is halted prior to a verdict being reached through no fault of the accused. Compare 10 U.S.C. §949h to Article 44 of the UCMJ, 10 U.S.C. §844.

[264] R.M.C. 907.

[265] *See also* CRS Report R40932, *Comparison of Rights in Military Commission Trials and Trials in Federal Criminal Court*, by Jennifer K. Elsea.

Chart 1. Comparison of Military Commission Rules

Authority

General Courts Martial	Military Commissions Act of 2006	Military Commissions Act of 2009
U.S. Constitution, Article I, §8, in particular cl. 14 "To make Rules for the Government and Regulation of the land and naval Forces."	U.S. Constitution, Article I, §8, in particular, cl. 10, "To define and punish Piracies and Felonies committed on the high Seas, and Offences against the Law of Nations"; cl. 11, "To declare War, grant Letters of Marque and Reprisal, and make Rules concerning Captures on Land and Water"; and cl. 14 (Necessary and Proper Clause).	Same as for MCA 2006.

Procedure

General Courts Martial	Military Commissions Act of 2006	Military Commissions Act of 2009
Rules are provided by the Uniform Code of Military Justice (UCMJ), chapter 47, Title 10, and the Rules for Courts-Martial (R.C.M.) and the Military Rules of Evidence (Mil. R. Evid.), issued by the President pursuant to art. 36, UCMJ, 10 U.S.C. §836.	The Secretary of Defense may prescribe rules of evidence and procedure for military commissions not inconsistent with the MCA. Rules applicable to courts-martial under the UCMJ are to apply except as otherwise specified. Former 10 U.S.C. §949a(a). The Secretary of Defense, in consultation with the Attorney General, may make exceptions to UCMJ procedural rules "as may be required by the unique circumstances of the conduct of military and intelligence operations during hostilities or by other practical need." Former 10 U.S.C.§949a(b). The rules must include certain rights as listed in former §949a(b)(2), but need not include procedural rules listed in former §949a(b)(3). Pursuant to the above authority, the Secretary of Defense published the Manual for Military Commissions (M.M.C.), including the Rules for Military Commissions (R.M.C.) and the Military Commission Rules of Evidence (Mil. Comm. R. Evid.).	The Secretary of Defense may prescribe rules of procedure for military commissions. Such rules may not be inconsistent with the MCA. Procedural rules for general courts-martial are to apply unless the MCA or UCMJ provide otherwise. Consultation with the Attorney General is required only in cases of exceptions, which continue to be permissible "as may be required by the unique circumstances of the conduct of military and intelligence operations during hostilities or by other practical need." 10 U.S.C. §949a (as amended). Suppression of certain evidence is a required right rather than an optional rule (see Chart 2 specific rights). The right to representation by civilian counsel is included. The procedural rules may no longer provide that evidence shall be admissible if the military judge determines that it would have "probative value to a reasonable person." 10 U.S.C. §949a(b) (as amended).

Jurisdiction over Persons

General Courts Martial	Military Commissions Act of 2006	Military Commissions Act of 2009
Members of the armed forces, cadets, midshipmen, reservists while on inactive-duty training, members of the National Guard or Air National Guard when in federal service, prisoners of war in custody of the armed forces, civilian employees accompanying the armed forces in time of declared war or contingency operation, and certain others, including "persons within an area leased by or otherwise reserved or acquired for the use of the United States." As amended by the MCA 2009, it includes persons entitled to prisoner of war status who violate the laws of war, subsection (13) (as amended). 10 U.S.C. §802. Individuals who are subject to military tribunal jurisdiction under the law of war may also be tried by general court martial. 10 U.S.C. §818. Court-martial jurisdiction for law of war offenses committed by "any person" (whether or not subject to the UCMJ under 10 U.S.C. §802) does not deprive common law military commissions under the UCMJ of concurrent jurisdiction, but the language preserving military commission jurisdiction does not apply to those conducted under the MCA. 10 U.S.C. §821 (as amended by MCA 2006).	Any "alien unlawful combatant" is subject to trial by military commission. Former 10 U.S.C. §948c. An "unlawful enemy combatant" is "a person who has engaged in hostilities or who has purposefully and materially supported hostilities against the United States or its co-belligerents who is not a lawful enemy combatant (including a person who is part of the Taliban, Al Qaeda, or associated forces)"; or a person determined to be an unlawful enemy combatant by a CSRT or other competent tribunal established under the authority of the President or the Secretary of Defense, which determination is dispositive of status. Former 10 U.S.C. §§948a and 948d(c). "Lawful combatant" is defined in terms similar to the definition of prisoner of war in Art 4 (1-3) of the Geneva Convention for the Treatment of Prisoners of War (GPW), except that it does not include militias and volunteer forces that form part of the regular armed forces of a state, although these apparently would be covered if they meet the four conditions set forth in GPW art. 4(2) Former 10 U.S.C. §948a(2). R.M.C. 201 and 202 provide for jurisdictional requirements of military commissions in accordance with the MCA.	Any "alien unprivileged enemy belligerent" is subject to trial by military commission under the MCA. (The requirement in the original Senate bill that such persons had engaged in or supported hostilities against the United States was deleted in conference.) 10 U.S.C. §948c. The term `unprivileged enemy belligerent' is defined to mean "an individual (other than a privileged belligerent) who has engaged in hostilities against the United States or its coalition partners; or has purposefully and materially supported hostilities against the United States or its coalition partners.... " It also includes persons who were members of Al Qaeda at the time they commit an offense. "Privileged belligerent" means an individual who is entitled to prisoners of war status under one of the eight categories set forth in GPW Art. 4. 10 U.S.C. §948a(6-7). The term "coalition partners" has a definition similar to that of "co-belligerents" in the MCA 2006. It applies to states and armed forces directly engaged in hostilities along with the United States or providing direct operational support. to the United States. "Hostilities," previously undefined, now refers to "any conflict subject to the laws of war." 10 U.S.C. §948a.

Jurisdiction over Offenses

General Courts Martial	Military Commissions Act of 2006	Military Commissions Act of 2009
Any offenses made punishable by the UCMJ; offenses subject to trial by military tribunal under the law of war. 10 U.S.C. §818.	A military commission has jurisdiction to try any offense made punishable by the MCA or the law of war when committed by an alien unlawful enemy combatant before, on, or after September 11, 2001. Former 10 U.S.C. §948d(a). Offenses previously codified at 10 U.S.C. §§950q-w included the following: murder of protected persons; attacking civilians, civilian objects, or protected property; pillaging; denying quarter; taking hostages; employing poison or similar weapons; using protected persons or property as shields; torture, cruel or inhuman treatment; intentionally causing serious bodily injury; mutilating or maiming; murder in violation of the law of war; destruction of property in violation of the law of war; using treachery or perfidy; improperly using a flag of truce or distinctive emblem; intentionally mistreating a dead body; rape; sexual assault or abuse; hijacking or hazarding a vessel or aircraft; terrorism; providing material support for terrorism; wrongfully aiding the enemy; spying, contempt; perjury and obstruction of justice. Former 10 U.S.C. §950v. Conspiracy (§950v(b)(28)), attempts (§950t), and solicitation (§950u) to commit the defined acts are also punishable.	A military commission has jurisdiction over persons subject to the MCA for offenses made punishable by the MCA, arts. 104 and 106 of the UCMJ, or the law of war. Military commissions are expressly authorized to determine their own jurisdiction. 10 U.S.C. §948d. (Articles 104 and 106 of the UCMJ, however, state that they do not apply to military commissions under the MCA. 10 U.S.C. §§904 & 906). MCA offenses remain otherwise substantially unchanged, except that there is an express requirement that offenses occurred "in the context of and associated with hostilities." 10 U.S.C. §950p. The definition of "cruel or inhuman treatment" is modified to refer to treatment that constitutes a grave breach of common Article 3 of the Geneva Conventions, regardless of where the crime takes place or the nationality of the victim. (The previous definition, which was codified at 10 U.S.C. §950v(b)(12), referred to 18 U.S.C. §2340(2).) 10 U.S.C. §950t(12).

Composition

General Courts Martial	Military Commissions Act of 2006	Military Commissions Act of 2009
A military judge and not less than five members, or if requested, except in capital cases, a military judge alone. 10 U.S.C. §816, R.C.M. 501.	A military judge and at least 5 members, unless the death penalty is sought, in which case no fewer than 12 members must be included. Former 10 U.S.C. §948m. Former 10 U.S.C. §949m provided that, in death penalty cases where 12 members were not reasonably available because of physical conditions or military exigencies, the convening authority may approve a commission with as few as 9 members.	No changes. 10 U.S.C. §948m; 10 U.S.C. §949m.

Chart 2. Comparison of Procedural Safeguards

Presumption of Innocence

General Courts Martial	Military Commissions Act of 2006	Military Commissions Act of 2009
If the defendant fails to enter a proper plea, a plea of not guilty will be entered. R.C.M. 910(b). Members of court-martial must be instructed that the "accused must be presumed to be innocent until the accused's guilt is established by legal and competent evidence beyond a reasonable doubt." R.C.M. 920(e). The accused shall be properly attired in uniform with grade insignia and any decorations to which entitled. Physical restraint shall not be imposed unless prescribed by the military judge. R.C.M. 804.	Before a vote is taken on the findings, the military judge must instruct the commission members "that the accused must be presumed to be innocent until his guilt is established by legal and competent evidence beyond reasonable doubt." 10 U.S.C. §949*l*. If an accused refuses to enter a plea or pleads guilty but provides inconsistent testimony, or if it appears that he lacks proper understanding of the meaning and effect of the guilty plea, the commission must treat the plea as denying guilt. 10 U.S.C. §949i.	10 U.S.C. §949*l* and 10 U.S.C. §949i are substantially unchanged.

Right to Remain Silent (Freedom from Coerced Statements)

General Courts Martial	Military Commissions Act of 2006	The Military Commissions Act of 2009
Coerced confessions or confessions made in custody without statutory equivalent of Miranda warning are not admissible as evidence. Art. 31, UCMJ, 10 U.S.C. §831. Rules of evidence provide that in most cases "an involuntary statement or any derivative evidence therefrom may not be received in evidence against an accused who made the statement if the accused makes a timely motion to suppress or an objection to the evidence under this rule." Mil. R. Evid. 304. The prosecutor must notify the defense of any incriminating statements made by the accused that are relevant to the case prior to the arraignment. Motions to suppress such statements must be made prior to pleading.	Sections a, b, and d of Article 31, UCMJ, were expressly made inapplicable. These provide that no person subject to the UCMJ may compel any person to incriminate himself or interrogate an accused without first informing him of his right to remain silent, and that statements obtained in violation of the above or through other unlawful inducement may not be received in evidence against him in a trial by court-martial. Former 10 U.S.C. §948b(d). Secretary of Defense permitted to provide that confessions allegedly elicited through coercion or compulsory self-incrimination that were otherwise admissible were not to be excluded at trial except when admission would violate Section 948r.	10 U.S.C. §948b(d) remains unchanged. Secretary of Defense may provide that confessions allegedly elicited through coercion or compulsory self-incrimination that are otherwise admissible are not to be excluded at trial unless their admission violates Section 948r. 10 U.S.C. §949a(b)(3)(B). Section 948r now provides for the exclusion of statements elicited through torture as well as cruel, inhuman, or degrading treatment prohibited by Section 1003 of the DTA (42 U.S.C. §2000dd), regardless of when the statement was made. No statement of the accused is admissible at trial unless the military judge finds that the totality of the circumstances renders the statement reliable and possessing sufficient

General Courts Martial	Military Commissions Act of 2006	The Military Commissions Act of 2009
Mil. R. Evid. 304. Interrogations conducted by foreign officials do not require warnings or presence of counsel unless the interrogation is instigated or conducted by U.S. military personnel. Mil. R. Evid. 305.	Former 10 U.S.C. §949a(b)(2)(C). Section 948r provided that statements elicited through torture may not be entered into evidence except to prove a charge of torture. A statement of the accused obtained prior to the enactment of the DTA through coercion that does not amount to torture was admissible if the military judge found that 1. the "totality of circumstances under which [it] was made renders it reliable and possessing sufficient probative value" and 2. "the interests of justice would best be served" by admission of the statement. Statements taken after passage of the DTA were admissible if the military judge also found that "the interrogation methods used to obtain [them] do not violate the cruel, unusual, or inhumane treatment or punishment prohibited by the Fifth, Eighth, and Fourteenth Amendments to the U.S. Constitution." Former 10 U.S.C. §948r. Evidence derived from impermissible interrogation methods was not expressly barred.	probative value and that it was either made incident to military operations, where the interests of justice would best be served by admission of the statement into evidence; or that the statement was voluntarily given, taking into consideration all relevant circumstances, including military and intelligence operations during hostilities; the accused's age, education level, military training; and the change in place or identity of interrogator between that statement and any prior questioning of the accused. 10 U.S.C. §949r. Derivative evidence obtained using coerced statement is not expressly barred.

Freedom from Unreasonable Searches and Seizures

General Courts Martial	Military Commissions Act of 2006	Military Commissions Act of 2009
"Evidence obtained as a result of an unlawful search or seizure ... is inadmissible against the accused ..." unless certain exceptions apply. Mil. R. Evid. 311. "Authorization to search" may be oral or written, and may be issued by a military judge or an officer in command of the area to be searched, or if the area is not under military control, with authority over persons subject to military law or the law of war. It must be based on probable cause. Mil. R. Evid. 315. Interception of wire and oral communications within the United States requires judicial application in accordance with 18 U.S.C. §§2516 et seq. Mil. R. Evid. 317. A search conducted by foreign officials is unlawful only if the accused is subject to "gross and brutal treatment." Mil. R. Evid. 311(c).	Not provided. Evidence was generally permitted if it was judged to have probative value to a reasonable person, unless it was obtained under circumstances that would render it unreliable. Former 10 U.S.C. §§948r, 949a. Procedural rules may provide that evidence gathered without authorization or a search warrant may be admitted into evidence. Former 10 U.S.C. §949a.	The language permitting procedural rules to permit evidence having probative value to a reasonable person was omitted. The Secretary of Defense may provide that "evidence seized outside the United States shall not be excluded from trial by military commission on the grounds that the evidence was not seized pursuant to a search warrant or other authorization." 10 U.S.C. §949a.

Effective Assistance of Counsel

General Courts Martial	Military Commissions Act of 2006	Military Commissions Act of 2009
The defendant has a right to military counsel at government expense. The defendant may choose counsel, if that attorney is reasonably available, and may hire a civilian attorney in addition to military counsel. Art. 38, UCMJ, 10 U.S.C. §838. Appointed counsel must be certified as qualified and may not be someone who has taken any part in the investigation or prosecution, unless explicitly requested by the defendant. Art. 27, UCMJ, 10 U.S.C. §827. The attorney-client privilege is honored. Mil. R. Evid. 502. Defense counsel must be a member of the bar of a federal or state court or authorized by a recognized licensing authority to practice law who is found by the military judge to be qualifed. R.C.M. 502. Once an attorney-client relationship has been formed, defense counsel can withdraw or be excused only at the request of the accused or on good cause shown. R.C.M. 506.	At least one qualifying military defense counsel is to be detailed "as soon as practicable after the swearing of charges…." Former 10 U.S.C. §948k. The accused may also hire a civilian attorney who 1. is a U.S. citizen, 2. is admitted to the bar in any state, district, or possession, 3. has never been disciplined, 4. has a SECRET clearance (or higher, if necessary for a particular case), and 5. agrees to comply with all applicable rules. Former 10 U.S.C. §949c(b)(3). If civilian counsel is hired, the detailed military counsel serves as associate counsel. Former 10 U.S.C. §949c(b)(5). No attorney-client privilege is mentioned. Adverse personnel actions may not be taken against defense attorneys because of the "zeal with which such officer, in acting as counsel, represented any accused before a military commission…." Former 10 U.S.C. §949b.	At least one qualifying military defense counsel is to be detailed "as soon as practicable." 10 U.S.C. §948k. The accused is entitled to select one "reasonably available" military counsel to represent him. The accused is not entitled to have more than one military counsel, but "associate defense counsel" may be authorized pursuant to regulations. 10 U.S.C. §§948c, 948k. 10 U.S.C. §949c, as it relates to the hiring of civilian counsel, remains substantially unchanged. 10 U.S.C. §949b, prohibiting adverse personnel actions against defense attorneys due to "the zeal with which such officer, in acting as counsel, represented any accused before a military commission ..." also remains unchanged. In capital cases, the accused is entitled to be represented, "to the greatest extent practicable, by at least one additional counsel who is learned in applicable law," who may be a civilian and may be compensated by the government in accordance with regulations. 10 U.S.C. §949a.

Right to Indictment and Presentment

General Courts Martial	Military Commissions Act of 2006	Military Commissions Act of 2009
The right to indictment by grand jury is explicitly excluded in "cases arising in the land or naval forces." Amendment V. UCMJ Article 32 provides for an inquiry similar to grand jury proceedings in federal criminal court. 10 U.S.C. §832. Whenever an offense is alleged, the commander is responsible for initiating a preliminary inquiry and deciding how to dispose of the offense. R.C.M. 303-06.	UCMJ Article 32 hearings are expressly made inapplicable. Former 10 U.S.C. §948b(d)(1)(C). Charges and specifications against an accused must be signed by a person subject to UCMJ swearing under oath that the signer has "personal knowledge of, or reason to believe, the matters set forth therein," and that they are "true in fact to the best of his knowledge and belief." The accused is to be informed of the charges and specifications against him as soon as practicable after charges are sworn. Former 10 U.S.C. §948q.	No substantial change to relevant sections of the MCA 2006. 10 U.S.C. §948b(d)(1)(C); 10 U.S.C. §948q.

Right to Written Statement of Charges

General Courts Martial	Military Commissions Act of 2006	Military Commissions Act of 2009
Charges and specifications must be signed under oath and made known to the accused as soon as practicable. Art. 30, UCMJ, 10 U.S.C. §830.	The trial counsel assigned is responsible for serving defense counsel a copy of the charges upon the accused, in English and, if appropriate, in another language that the accused understands, "sufficiently in advance of trial to prepare a defense." Former 10 U.S.C. §948s.	No substantial change to relevant sections of the MCA 2006. 10 U.S.C. §948s.

Right to Be Present at Trial

General Courts Martial	Military Commissions Act of 2006	Military Commissions Act of 2009
The presence of the accused is required during arraignment, at the plea, and at every stage of the court-martial unless the accused waives the right by voluntarily absenting him or herself from the proceedings after the arraignment or by persisting in conduct that justifies the trial judge in ordering the removal of the accused from the proceedings. R.C.M. 804.	The accused has the right to be present at all sessions of the military commission except deliberation or voting, unless exclusion of the accused is permitted under §949d. Former 10 U.S.C. §949a(b)(1)(B). The accused may be excluded from attending portions of the proceeding if the military judge determines that the accused persists in disruptive or dangerous conduct. Former 10 U.S.C. §949d(e).	No substantial change to relevant sections of the MCA 2006. 10 U.S.C. §949a(b)(2)(B); 10 U.S.C. §949d(d).

Prohibition Against Ex Post Facto Crimes

General Courts Martial	Military Commissions Act of 2006	Military Commissions Act of 2009
Courts-martial will not enforce an ex post facto law, including one that increases the amount of pay to be forfeited for a specific crime. U.S. v. Gorki, 47 M.J. 370 (1997).	Crimes punishable by military commissions under the new chapter were codified in subchapter VII. It included the crime of conspiracy, which a plurality of the Supreme Court in *Hamdan v. Rumsfeld* viewed as invalid as a charge of war crimes. 548 U.S. 557 (2006). The act declared that it "codif[ies] offenses that have traditionally been triable by military commissions," and that "because the [defined crimes] (including provisions that incorporate definitions in other provisions of law) are declarative of existing law, they do not preclude trial for crimes that occurred before the date of enactment." Former 10 U.S.C. §950p. The statute expressly provided jurisdiction over the defined crimes, whether committed prior to, on or after September 11, 2001. Former 10 U.S.C. §948d(a).	The definition of crimes is contained in Subchapter VIII. The conspiracy charge remains available under 10 U.S.C. §950t(29). The D.C. Circuit upheld a conspiracy conviction on the basis that such a charge was not plainly historically unavailable at military commission trials. Al Bahlul v. United States, __*F3d.* __ *(D.C. Cir. 2014)(en banc).* The charge of "material support for terrorism," is now codified at 10 U.S.C. §950t(25). The D.C. Circuit has invalidated convictions for material support on the basis that it was not a war crime when committed. Hamdan v. United States, 696 F.3d 1238 (D.C. Cir. 2012) (*Hamdan II*); Al Bahlul v. United States, __*F3d.* __ *(D.C. Cir. 2014)(en banc).* 10 U.S.C. §950p continues to declare that the MCA as amended does not define new crimes, but rather codifies preexisting offenses for trial by military commission, which offenses "have traditionally been triable under the law of war or otherwise triable by military commission," and therefore "does not preclude trial for offenses that occurred before the date of the enactment.... " 10 U.S.C. §950p(d). Offenses that were clearly not violations of the law of war when committed nor traditionally triable by military commission are not prosecutable by military commission under the MCA. *Al Bahlul v. United States, __F3d. __ (D.C. Cir. 2014 (en banc).* Section 948d continues to provide for jurisdiction over crimes committed "prior to, on or after September 11, 2001," although the offense must have been committed "in the context of and associated with hostilities." 10 U.S.C. §948d; 10 U.S.C. §950p.

Protection Against Double Jeopardy

General Courts Martial	Military Commissions Act of 2006	Military Commissions Act of 2009
Double jeopardy clause applies. See Wade v. Hunter, 336 US 684, 688-89 (1949). Art. 44, UCMJ prohibits former jeopardy, provides for jeopardy to attach after introduction of evidence, or in cases resulting in a finding of guilty, after review of the case has been completed. 10 U.S.C. §844. General court-martial proceeding is considered to be a federal trial for double jeopardy purposes. Double jeopardy does not result from charges brought in state or foreign courts, although court-martial in such cases is disfavored. U. S. v. Stokes, 12 M.J. 229 (C.M.A. 1982). Once military authorities have turned service member over to civil authorities for trial, military may have waived jurisdiction for that crime, although it may be possible to charge the individual for another crime arising from the same conduct. See 54 AM. JUR. 2d, Military and Civil Defense §§227-28. In cases in which a rehearing is ordered, the accused may not be tried for any offense of which he was found not guilty, and a sentence cannot be increased unless there is a finding of guilty of an offense not considered in the original proceedings or the sentence prescribed for the offense is mandatory. Art. 63, UCMJ, 10 U.S.C. §863. The United States may not appeal an order or ruling that amounts to a finding of not guilty. Art. 62, UCMJ, 10 U.S.C. §862.	"No person may, without his consent, be tried by a military commission a second time for the same offense." Jeopardy attaches when a guilty finding becomes final after review of the case has been completed. There is no indication when jeopardy attaches in cases that are dismissed without any fault of the accused. Former 10 U.S.C. §949h. The United States may not appeal an order or ruling that amounts to a finding of not guilty. Former 10 U.S.C. §950d(a)(2). The convening authority may not revise findings or order a rehearing in any case to reconsider a finding of not guilty of any specification or a ruling which amounts to a finding of not guilty, or reconsider a finding of not guilty of any charge, unless there has been a finding of guilty under a specification laid under that charge, which sufficiently alleges a violation. The convening authority may not increase the severity of the sentence unless the sentence prescribed for the offense is mandatory. Former 10 U.S.C. §950b(d)(2)(B).	No substantial change in 10 U.S.C. §949h. The United States may not appeal any finding of not guilty. 10 U.S.C. §950d(b). Limitations on the convening authority's ability to revise findings or order a rehearing are unchanged. 10 U.S.C. §950b(d)(2)(B).

Speedy and Public Trial

General Courts Martial	Military Commissions Act of 2006	Military Commissions Act of 2009
In general, accused must be brought to trial within 120 days of the preferral of charges or the imposition of restraint, whichever date is earliest. R.C.M. 707(a). The right to a public trial applies in courts-martial but is not absolute. R.C.M. 806. The military trial judge may exclude the public from portions of a proceeding for the purpose of protecting classified information if the prosecution demonstrates an overriding need to do so and the closure is no broader than necessary. United States v. Grunden, 2 M.J. 116 (CMA 1977).	There is no right to a speedy trial. Article 10, UCMJ, 10 U.S.C. §810, is expressly made inapplicable to military commissions. Former 10 U.S.C. §948b(d). The military judge may close all or part of a trial to the public only after making a determination that such closure is necessary to protect information, the disclosure of which would be harmful to national security interests or to the physical safety of any participant. Former 10 U.S.C. §949d(d).	No substantial change to relevant sections of the MCA. 10 U.S.C. §948b(d); 10 U.S.C. §949b(c).

Burden and Standard of Proof

General Courts Martial	Military Commissions Act of 2006	Military Commissions Act of 2009
Members of court martial must be instructed that the burden of proof to establish guilt is upon the government and that any reasonable doubt must be resolved in favor of the defendant. R.C.M. 920(e).	Commission members are to be instructed that the accused is presumed to be innocent until his "guilt is established by legal and competent evidence beyond reasonable doubt"; that any reasonable doubt as to the guilt of the accused must result in acquittal; that reasonable doubt as to the degree of guilt must be resolved in favor of the lower degree as to which there is no reasonable doubt; and that the burden of proof is on the government. Former 10 U.S.C. §949*l*. Two-thirds of the members must concur on a finding of guilty, except in capital cases. (The death penalty requires a unanimous finding as to guilt as well as sentence). Former 10 U.S.C. §949m. The Secretary of Defense may prescribe that the military judge is to exclude any evidence, the probative value of which is substantially outweighed by the danger of unfair prejudice, confusion of the issues, or misleading the members of the commission, or by considerations of undue delay, waste of time, or needless presentation of cumulative evidence. Former 10 U.S.C. §949a.	Instructions for commission members on the burden of and standard of proof are unchanged. 10 U.S.C. §949*l*. Two-thirds of the members must concur on a finding of guilty, except in capital cases. 10 U.S.C. §949m. The provision for the exclusion of irrelevant, cumulative, or prejudicial evidence is expressly made a right of the accused rather than an optional rule subject to the discretion of the Secretary of Defense. 10 U.S.C. §949a(b)(2)(E-F).

Privilege Against Self-Incrimination (Freedom from Compelled Testimony)

General Courts Martial	Military Commissions Act of 2006	Military Commissions Act of 2009
No person subject to the UCMJ may compel any person to answer incriminating questions. Art. 31(a) UCMJ, 10 U.S.C. §831(a). Defendant may not be compelled to give testimony that is immaterial or potentially degrading. Art. 31(c), UCMJ, 10 U.S.C. §831(c). No adverse inference is to be drawn from a defendant's refusal to answer any questions or testify at court-martial. Mil. R. Evid. 301(f). Witnesses may not be compelled to give testimony that may be incriminating unless granted immunity for that testimony by a general court-martial convening authority, as authorized by the Attorney General, if required. 18 U.S.C. §6002; R.C.M. 704.	"No person shall be required to testify against himself at a commission proceeding." Former 10 U.S.C. §948r(a). While most of Art. 31, UCMJ, relating to compelled self-incrimination, is declared inapplicable, Art. 31(c), UCMJ, related to immaterial or degrading statements or evidence, applies to all military tribunals. Former 10 U.S.C. §948b(d)(1)(B). Adverse inferences drawn from a failure to testify are not expressly prohibited; however, members are to be instructed that "the accused must be presumed to be innocent until his guilt is established by legal and competent evidence." Former 10 U.S.C. §949*l*(c). There does not appear to be a provision for immunity of witnesses, although 18 U.S.C. §6002 appears to apply.	No substantial change in relevant sections of the MCA 2006. 10 U.S.C. §948r(b); 10 U.S.C. §948b(d)(1)(B), 10 U.S.C. §949*l*(c).

Right to Examine or Have Examined Adverse Witnesses (Hearsay and Classified Evidence)

General Courts Martial	Military Commissions Act of 2006	Military Commissions Act of 2009
Rules of Evidence prohibit generally the introduction at trial of statements made out of court to prove the truth of the matter stated unless the declarant is available for cross-examination at trial (hearsay rule). Mil. R. Evid. 801 *et seq.* Exceptions exist for cases in which the statement may be presumed to be reliable due to specific circumstances (Rule 803) or the witness is unavailable in court (Rule 804). There is also a "residual exception" (Rule 807), which covers statements not covered under other rules but having	"Defense counsel may cross-examine each witness for the prosecution who testifies before the commission." Former 10 U.S.C. §949c(b)(7). The Secretary of Defense had the authority to establish that hearsay evidence not admissible under the rules of evidence applicable in trial by general courts-martial is admissible only if the proponent notifies the adverse party sufficiently in advance of its intention to offer the evidence and the particulars of the evidence (including information on the general circumstances under which	The right to cross-examine witnesses remains unchanged. 10 U.S.C. §949c(b)(6). The Secretary of Defense is permitted to provide that hearsay evidence that would not be admissible at a general court-martial is admissible if adequate notice is given and the military judge determines that the statement is reliable and is offered as evidence of a material fact, that direct testimony from the witness is not available or would have an adverse impact on military or intelligence operations, and that the general purposes of the rules of evidence and the interests of justice will best be served by admission of the

General Courts Martial	Military Commissions Act of 2006	Military Commissions Act of 2009
similar indicia of trustworthiness. Such statements are admissible if notice is provided to the adverse party sufficient to provide a fair opportunity to prepare to rebut it, and if the military judge determines the statement is more probative of the material fact for which it is offered than other reasonably available evidence and that its admission would serve the interests of justice. Mil. R. Evid. 801 *et seq.* In capital cases, sworn depositions may not be used in lieu of witness, unless court-martial is treated as non-capital or it is introduced by the defense. Art. 49, UCMJ, 10 U.S.C. §849.	the evidence was obtained), unless the party opposing the admission of the evidence "clearly demonstrates that the evidence is unreliable or lacking in probative value." Former 10 U.S.C. §949a(b)(2)(E). In the case of classified information, the military judge could authorize the government to delete specified portions of evidence to be made available to the accused, or allow an unclassified summary or statement setting forth the facts the evidence would tend to prove, to the extent practicable in accordance with the rules used at general courts-martial. Former 10 U.S.C. §949d(f)(2)(A).	statement into evidence. In determining reliability, the military judge may be obligated to consider the degree to which the statement is corroborated, the indicia of reliability within the statement itself, and whether the will of the declarant was overborne, 10 U.S.C. §949a(b)(3)(D). The burden of persuasion to demonstrate unreliability or lack of probative value appears to be on the profferer of the evidence. (Language providing otherwise was repealed.) The protection of classified information is governed by subchapter V, 10 U.S.C. §§949p-1–949p-7. Subchapter V provides that the government cannot be compelled to disclose classified information to anyone not authorized to receive it. If the government claims a privilege, the military judge may not authorize the discovery of or access to the classified information unless he determines the evidence is noncumulative, relevant, and helpful to a legally cognizable defense, rebuttal of the prosecution's case, or to sentencing. If the military judge determines disclosure or access is necessary, the military judge must grant the government's request to delete or withhold specified items of classified information; to substitute a summary for classified information; or to substitute a statement admitting relevant facts that the classified information or material would tend to prove, so long as the alternative procedure would provide the accused with substantially the same ability to make a defense. If the prosecution makes a motion for protective measures in camera, the accused has no opportunity to request a reconsideration.

Right to Compulsory Process to Obtain Witnesses and Other Evidence (Discovery)

General Courts Martial	Military Commissions Act of 2006	Military Commissions Act of 2009
Defendants before court-martial have the right to compel appearance of witnesses necessary to their defense. R.C.M. 703. Process to compel witnesses in court-martial cases is to be similar to the process used in federal courts. Moreover, the defense and prosecution "shall have equal opportunity to obtain witnesses and other evidence." Art. 46, UCMJ, 10 U.S.C. §846. In the case of a witness who is not available to testify, but whose testimony is essential to a fair trial, and no adequate substitution for the testimony can be provided, the judge must grant appropriate relief, unless the unavailability of the witness is the fault of the requesting party. R.C.M. 703. There is authority to grant immunity to witnesses in order to compel testimony that may incriminate the witness. 18 U.S.C. §6002; R.C.M. 704. The prosecution is required to disclose any sworn statements that are material to the case. The government must also provide results or reports of any physical or mental examination of the defendant. Upon the request of the accused, the government must permit the accused to inspect and make copies or photos of tangible objects, buildings or places, within the control of military authorities if (i) the item is material to preparing the defense; (ii) the government intends to use the item in its case-in-chief at trial; or (iii) the item was obtained from or belongs to the defendant.	Defense counsel is to be afforded a reasonable opportunity to obtain witnesses and other evidence, including evidence in the possession of the United States, according to DOD regulations. Former 10 U.S.C. §949j(a). The military commission is authorized to compel witnesses under U.S. jurisdiction to appear. Former 10 U.S.C. §949j(b). The trial counsel is obligated to disclose exculpatory evidence of which he is aware to the defense, but such information, if classified, is available to the accused only in a redacted or summary form, and only if making the information available is possible without compromising intelligence sources, methods, or activities, or other national security interests. Former 10 U.S.C. §949j(d). The military judge may authorize discovery in accordance with rules prescribed by the Secretary of Defense to redact classified information or to provide an unclassified summary or statement describing the evidence. Former 10 U.S.C. §949j(c).	Defense counsel is to be afforded a reasonable opportunity to obtain witnesses and other evidence, including evidence in the possession of the United States, in a manner comparable to the opportunity available to a criminal defendant in federal court. As previously, the military commission is authorized to compel witnesses under U.S. jurisdiction to appear. This may include the authority to grant immunity to witnesses whose testimony is self-incriminatory. 10 U.S.C.§949j(a)(as amended). Congress emphasized its sense that "the fairness and effectiveness of the military commissions system under chapter 47A of title 10 ... will depend to a significant degree on the adequacy of defense counsel and associated resources for individuals accused, particularly in the case of capital cases," and that "defense counsel in military commission cases, particularly in capital cases, ... should be fully resourced as provided.... " FY2010 NDAA, §1807. The obligation to disclose exculpatory information is expanded to include mitigating evidence, and the obligation extends beyond information known to the trial counsel to include all information that is known or reasonably should be known to any government officials who participated in the investigation and prosecution of the case against the defendant. The military judge may authorize trial counsel to disclose such information in a redacted or summary form, and shall authorize such alternative forms evidence when consistent with the interests of justice. 10 U.S.C. §949j(b). The provisions regarding the production of classified information are removed from §949(d) and revised provisions inserted in

General Courts Martial	Military Commissions Act of 2006	Military Commissions Act of 2009
Trial counsel (the prosecution) must give notice of any witnesses it intends to call at trial. Exculpatory or mitigating evidence known to trial counsel must also be disclosed. R.C.M. 701. Either party can request approval for expert testimony from the convening authority, whose denial can be overridden by the military judge on a finding that such testimony is necessary and relevant. R.C.M. 703(d). Discovery involving classified information is governed by Mil. R. Evid. 505.		subchapter V, which is to be construed consistent with the Classified Information Procedures Act (18 U.S.C. App.) to the extent that such a construction does not conflict with the revised provisions. 10 U.S.C. §949p-1. The military judge is to issue a protection order to prevent the disclosure of any classified information that has been disclosed or otherwise obtained by the accused. 10 U.S.C. §949p-3.

Right to Trial by Impartial Judge

General Courts Martial	Military Commissions Act of 2006	Military Commissions Act of 2009
A qualified military judge is detailed to preside over the court-martial. The convening authority may not prepare or review any report concerning the performance or effectiveness of the military judge. Art. 26, UCMJ, 10 U.S.C. §826. UCMJ Article 37 prohibits unlawful influence of courts-martial through admonishment, censure, or reprimand of its members by the convening authority or commanding officer, or any unlawful attempt by a person subject to the UCMJ to coerce or influence the action of a court-martial or convening authority. Art. 37, UCMJ, 10 U.S.C. §837.	Military judges must take an oath to perform their duties faithfully. Former 10 U.S.C. §949g. The convening authority is prohibited from preparing or reviewing any report concerning the effectiveness, fitness, or efficiency of a military judge. Former 10 U.S.C. §948j(a). A military judge may not be assigned to a case in which he is the accuser, an investigator, a witness, or a counsel. Former 10 U.S.C. §948j(c). The military judge may not consult with the members of the commission except in the presence of the accused, trial counsel, and defense counsel, nor may he vote with the members of the commission. Former 10 U.S.C. §948j(d). Convening authority may not censure, reprimand, or admonish the military judge. No person may attempt to coerce or use unauthorized means to influence the action of a commission.	No substantial change from relevant sections of the MCA 2006. 10 U.S.C. §949g; 10 U.S.C. §948j(f); 10 U.S.C. §948j(c); 10 U.S.C. §948j(d); 10 U.S.C. §949b; 10 U.S.C. §949f.

General Courts Martial	Military Commissions Act of 2006	Military Commissions Act of 2009
	Former 10 U.S.C. §949b. The military judge may be challenged for cause. Former 10 U.S.C. §949f.	

Right to Trial by Impartial Jury

General Courts Martial	Military Commissions Act of 2006	Military Commissions Act of 2009
A military accused has no Sixth Amendment right to a trial by petit jury. *Ex Parte* Quirin, 317 U.S. 1, 39-40 (1942) (dicta). However, "Congress has provided for trial by members at a court-martial." United States v. Witham, 47 M.J. 297, 301 (1997); Art. 25, UCMJ, 10 U.S.C. §825. The Sixth Amendment requirement that the jury be impartial applies to court-martial members and covers not only the selection of individual jurors, but also their conduct during the trial proceedings and the subsequent deliberations. United States v. Lambert, 55 M.J. 293 (2001). The absence of a right to trial by jury precludes criminal trial of civilians by court-martial. Reid v. Covert, 354 U.S. 1 (1957); Kinsella v. United States *ex rel.* Singleton, 361 U.S. 234 (1960).	Military commission members must take an oath to perform their duties faithfully. Former 10 U.S.C. §949g. The accused may make one peremptory challenge, and may challenge other members for cause. Former 10 U.S.C. §949f. No convening authority may censure, reprimand, or admonish the commission or any member with respect to the findings or sentence or the exercise of any other functions in the conduct of the proceedings. No person may attempt to coerce or, by any unauthorized means, influence the action of a commission or any member thereof, in reaching the findings or sentence in any case. Military commission duties may not be considered in the preparation of an effectiveness report or any similar document with potential impact on career-advancement. Former 10 U.S.C. §949b.	No substantial change from relevant sections of the MCA 2006. 10 U.S.C. §949g; 10 U.S.C. §949f; 10 U.S.C. §949b.

Right to Appeal to Independent Reviewing Authority

General Courts Martial	Military Commissions Act of 2006	Military Commissions Act of 2009
The accused may submit matters concerning the findings and the sentence for consideration by the convening authority. The convening authority may approve, disapprove, commute, or suspend the sentence in whole or in part, set aside a finding of guilty or change a finding of guilty to a charge or specification to	The accused may submit matters for consideration by the convening authority with respect to the authenticated findings or sentence of the military commission. The convening authority must review timely submissions prior to taking action.	No change in 10 U.S.C. §950b. The accused may appeal a final decision of the military commission with respect to any properly raised issue to the United States Court of Military Commission Review (USCMCR), a body composed of judges who meet the same

General Courts Martial	Military Commissions Act of 2006	Military Commissions Act of 2009
a finding of guilty to an offense that is a lesser included offense of the offense stated in the charge or specification. Art. 60, UCMJ, 10 U.S.C. §860. Certain judgments of courts-martial, depending on the severity of the sentence, are directly appealable to the respective Service's Court of Criminal Appeals, which reviews the findings and sentence as approved by the convening authority, considering questions of both fact and law. In the event it sets aside a judgment, it may order a rehearing unless its act was based on insufficiency of evidence in the record to support the findings, in which case it must order a dismissal. Art. 66, UCMJ, 10 U.S.C. §866. The accused may petition for review of a Court of Criminal Appeals decision to the Court of Appeals for the Armed Forces, a court of civilian judges that is empowered to act only with respect to matters of law. Art. 67, UCMJ, 10 U.S.C. §867. CAAF decisions, other than denials to hear a case, may be appealed to the Supreme Court through writ of certiorari. Art. 67a, UCMJ, 10 U.S.C. §867a. The writ of habeas corpus provides the primary means by which those sentenced by military court, having exhausted military appeals, can challenge a conviction or sentence in a civilian court. The scope of matters that a court will address is narrower than in challenges of federal or state convictions. Burns v. Wilson, 346 U.S. 137 (1953).	Former 10 U.S.C. §950b. The accused may appeal a final decision of the military commission with respect to issues of law to the Court of Military Commission Review, a body composed of appellate military judges who meet the same qualifications as military judges or comparable qualifications for civilian judges. Former 10 U.S.C. §950f. Once these appeals are exhausted, the accused may appeal the final decision to the United States Court of Appeals for the District of Columbia Circuit, which is limited to reviewing questions of law regarding "whether the final decision was consistent with the standards and procedures specified in [the MCA] and to the extent applicable, the Constitution and the laws of the United States." D.C. Cir. appellate decisions may be reviewed by the Supreme Court under writ of certiorari. Former 10 U.S.C. §950g. Other review by a civilian court, including review on petition of habeas corpus, is expressly prohibited. Former 10 U.S.C. §950j (likely unconstitutional under Boumediene v. Bush, 533 U.S. 723 (2008)(holding §7 of the MCA to be invalid suspension of the writ of habeas corpus)).	qualifications as military judges or comparable qualifications for civilian judges. The Secretary of Defense may appoint persons already serving as appellate military judges to the USCMCR, or the President may appoint judges subject to Senate advice and consent. 10 U.S.C. §950f. Once these appeals are exhausted, the accused may appeal the final decision to the United States Court of Appeals for the District of Columbia Circuit, with respect to the findings and sentence as approved by the convening authority and as affirmed or set aside as incorrect in law by the USCMCR. The appellate court may take action only with respect to matters of law, including the sufficiency of the evidence to support the verdict. D.C. Cir. appellate decisions may be reviewed by the Supreme Court under writ of certiorari. 10 U.S.C. §950g. Other review by a civilian court, including review on petition of habeas corpus, is no longer expressly prohibited.

Protection Against Excessive Penalties

General Courts Martial	Military Commissions Act of 2006	Military Commissions Act of 2009
Death may only be adjudged for certain crimes where the defendant is found guilty by unanimous vote of court-martial members present at the time of the vote. Prior to arraignment, the trial counsel must give the defense written notice of aggravating factors the prosecution intends to prove. R.C.M. 1004. A conviction of spying during time of war under UMCJ Article 106 carries a mandatory death penalty. 10 U.S.C. §906. Cruel and unusual punishments are prohibited. Art. 55, UCMJ, 10 U.S.C. §855. In capital cases, "equal opportunity to obtain witnesses and other evidence" under Art. 46, UCMJ may entitle the accused to expert assistance at the Government's expense. United States v. Kreutzer, 61 M.J. 293 (CAAF 2005). If a sentence extends to death, dismissal, or a dishonorable or bad conduct discharge, that part of the sentence may not be executed until required approval is given and all appeals are exhausted or waived. Art. 71, UCMJ, 10 U.S.C. §871.	Military commissions may adjudge "any punishment not forbidden by [the MCA] or the law of war, including the penalty of death…." Former 10 U.S.C. §948d. A vote of two-thirds of the members present is required for sentences of up to 10 years. Longer sentences require the concurrence of three-fourths of the members present. The death penalty must be approved unanimously on a unanimous guilty verdict. Where the death penalty is sought, a panel of 12 members is required (unless not "reasonably available," in which case the minimum is nine members). The death penalty must be expressly authorized for the offense, and the charges must have expressly sought the penalty of death. Former 10 U.S.C. §949m. An accused who is sentenced to death may waive his appeal, but may not withdraw an appeal. Former 10 U.S.C. §950c. The death sentence may not be executed until the commission proceedings have been finally adjudged lawful and the time for filing a writ has expired or the writ has been denied; and the President approves the sentence. Former 10 U.S.C. §950i. In capital cases, the accused is not entitled to assistance of counsel with expertise in death penalty cases. Former 10 U.S.C. §949a (civilian counsel only authorized if provided at no expense of the government).	Few substantial changes from MCA 2006. 10 U.S.C. §949m; 10 U.S.C. §950i. In capital cases, the accused is entitled to assistance of counsel with expertise in death penalty cases, which may include civilian counsel paid for by the government. 10 U.S.C. §949a. In the case of a capital case in which the accused pleads guilty, the sentence must be approved unanimously by members present. 10 U.S.C. §949m. An accused who is sentenced to death may neither waive nor withdraw an appeal. 10 U.S.C. §950c.

Author Contact Information

Jennifer K. Elsea
Legislative Attorney
jelsea@crs.loc.gov, 7-5466

www.ingramcontent.com/pod-product-compliance
Lightning Source LLC
Chambersburg PA
CBHW080548290526
45790CB00006B/2591
* 9 7 8 1 5 0 8 7 0 0 2 0 3 *